Proverbs

The Subject of

Wisdom

A Powerful Teaching Guide

...Whoever finds [wisdom] finds life, and obtains favor from the LORD! (Proverbs 8:35)

Paul M. Schrader

This book is dedicated to my students Jessica, Rachel, Brittany, and Brandy who invited me into their Sunday School class, to my friend and mentor Joe Ann Roberts, and to her son Jeff. It is because of this most blessed time in my life that this book has become a reality.
*"Train up a child in the way he should go,
And when he is old he will not depart from it."*
(Proverbs 22:6)

"The Subject of Wisdom" (3rd Edition)
Copyright 2013
ISBN-13: 978-1482625707
ISBN-10: 1482625709
All Rights Reserved! No part of this material may be reproduced without expressed permission from the Author.

Additional copies and Volume Discounts available at
http://www.createspace.com/4185037

Proverbs

The Subject of Wisdom

Choices--life is full of them! Most are simple, and are made without much thought. Others are more difficult, and we take time to consider how a particular choice affects our lives and the lives of others. Sometimes we even consult God's Word when faced with a difficult choice. But how often do we actually search God's Word for guidance for the seemingly simple everyday choices?

As people of God we take our children to church, teach them about God, and hope that they will make Godly choices in life. We teach them salvation, the Ten Commandments, and stories of Adam and Eve, Noah, Moses, and other Biblical characters.

But do we really teach them what they will need to successfully face an ungodly world? It is my belief that of all the Biblical things we instill in them, we fail to *clearly* teach the *one thing* they will need *above all else* to *truly* succeed and live a life that is abundantly blessed by God...and that one thing is Wisdom!

Every day people make choices based on what they think and how they feel, and do so with the intention of being a *good person*. However, these same individuals often find themselves praying for God to rescue them from the bad situations in which they find themselves. Many times, those situations are the direct result of choices they made that do not line up with the principles of Wisdom found in God's Word. If even our simple choices were based on God's Wisdom, then the promises of God would occur more often in our lives.

Much of God's Wisdom was given to us by King Solomon and is found in the book of Proverbs. The difficulty I had studying Wisdom is the way it is distributed throughout the book. Some verses in Proverbs continue the same subject for a large part of a chapter. The difficulty for me came when the subject changed from verse to verse, or even changed within a single verse!

Each time I read Proverbs I came away with only a few new verses that I felt "spoke to me." I never felt I came away with a clear picture of any of the personas portrayed in Proverbs such as the Wise Man, the Righteous Man, the Foolish Man, or the Wicked Man. Clearly understanding these personas is essential to applying God's Wisdom to our daily lives.

Imagine trying to describe George Washington to someone who has never seen a picture of him. Reading Proverbs straight through can be like looking at a picture of George Washington that has been cut into several pieces, and then mixed with pieces of several other presidential pictures. It would make him difficult to describe. But if all of the pieces of George Washington's picture were put together and arranged in an order that makes sense, then it would certainly be much easier to describe him.

The purpose of this book is to help give a *clear* and *memorable* picture of each persona and subject that is also easy to reference. I took every verse of Proverbs and re-arranged them into categories by subject. This all-inclusive look at Proverbs is a simplified overview that makes Wisdom much easier to grasp and retain. Verses from other books of the Bible have also been added for a more complete overview on some subjects. Some words have been changed or added for subjective clarity or readability and are in brackets [ ], and some word endings changed to make them more timely. I have strived intently to keep from changing the meaning of any verse! (Proverbs 30:6)

The majority of the passages are from the New King James Version (**NKJV**) although the King James Version (**KJV**) was used for a few of the verses where I felt they had a deeper meaning. Verses from other books of the Bible are **KJV** unless otherwise noted.

Although the Proverbs are gender-specific, both men and women should learn the virtues or dangers of each persona portrayed. They are applicable and of value to all.

I also encourage you to read Proverbs from the Bible. In the original form, the Holy Spirit may bring thoughts to mind that you may not receive from the order given here. I have categorized the verses as I understand and interpret their meaning.

It is my hope and prayer that this book makes it much easier for you to grasp and apply the principles of Wisdom to your walk with God.

Paul M. Schrader

Proverbs by Subject

God   9
God the Creator
The Purposes of God
The Ways of God
Trusting God in Adversity
The Word of God

The Fear of the LORD   12

The Call to Wisdom, Knowledge & Understanding   13

Proverbs 1:   The Beginning of Knowledge
                    The Call of Wisdom
Proverbs 2:   The Value of Wisdom
Proverbs 3:   Guidance for the Young
Proverbs 4:   Security in Wisdom
Proverbs 6:   The Light of Wisdom
Proverbs 7:   Treasure Wisdom
Proverbs 8:   The Excellence of Wisdom
Proverbs 9:   The Way of Wisdom
Proverbs 19: The Value of Wisdom to the Soul
Proverbs 22: Sayings of the Wise
Proverbs 23: Give Your Heart to Wisdom
Proverbs 24: The Sweetness of Wisdom

The Ultimate Wisdom!

Chastening and Correction   24
The Chastening of the LORD
Correcting Children
The Rod of Correction

The Wise Person   26
The Wise Desire Instruction, Knowledge and Understanding
The Favor of the Wise
The Strength of Wisdom
The Prudent Man
The Wise Man Heeds Counsel
Rebuking the Wise

The Foolish Person   30
The Foolish Despise Wisdom, Knowledge and Understanding
Fools Delight in Sin *
A Fool Does Not See His Sin
The Foolish Lack Self-Control
Contending with the Foolish
The Shame of Foolishness
The Sorrow of a Fool's Parents
The Correction of Fools

The Righteous Person   33
The LORD Blesses the Righteous
God Hears the Prayers of the Righteous
Deliverance of the Righteous
The Root of the Righteous
The Honor and Integrity of the Righteous
The Thoughts of the Righteous
The Labor of the Righteous
The Glory of the Righteous
Sins of the Righteous

The Wicked Person   37
The Destruction of the Wicked
Notable Characteristics of the Wicked
The Path of the Wicked
The Wicked are Pure in Their Own Eyes
The Guilty Man
Shame of the Wicked

The Proud Person — 41

Abominations — 43

Riches and Poverty — 45
Not Too Rich, Not Too Poor
Diligence to Obtain Wealth
False Confidence in Riches
Contentment
Wealth Makes Many Friends
Giving
Considering the Poor
Do Not Oppress the Poor
Gain by Deceit
Fools and Their Money
The Bread of a Miser
Treasures in Heaven

The Slothful Person — 53
The Field of the Slothful
Consider the Ant
The Lazy Man

Debt and Surety — 56

Gifts and Bribes — 57

Greed — 58
Proverbs 1: Shun Evil Council
Hastening to be Rich

The Thief — 60

Friendship 61
Choosing Friends Wisely
Being a Friend
The Poor Man's Friends

Enemies and Strife 62
Strife with Neighbors
Enemies
Quarrels Not Your Own

The Words of a Person's Mouth 64
The Fruit of a Person's Words
The Mouth of the Wise and Foolish
The Mouth of the Righteous
The Mouth of the Wicked
Truth
Lies and Deceit
The False Witness
Gossip
Speaking Evil of Others
Self-Praise
Anger
Discernment
Vows

The Heart 73
Gladness and Sadness of the Heart
Plans of the Heart
God Searches the Heart
The Wise and Foolish Hearts
The Heart of the Wicked

Adultery and Fornication 77
Proverbs 5: The Peril of Adultery
Proverbs 6: Beware of Adultery
Proverbs 7: The Crafty Harlot
Proverbs 9: The Foolish Woman
Adultery of the Heart

Women   *83*
Finding a Wife
The Foolish Wife
The Contentious Wife
Proverbs 31: The Virtuous Wife

Wine   86

The King   88
The Good King
The Absence of a Wise Ruler
The King's Wrath and Favor
Friends of Rulers
Dining With Rulers
Further Wise Sayings of Solomon Concerning the King
The Words of King Lemuel

The Wisdom of Agur   92
The Man Without Wisdom
Four Things Never Satisfied
Four Things Beyond Understanding
Four Things Unbearable
Four Things Exceedingly Wise
Four Things Majestic

God

There is no wisdom or understanding
  Or counsel against the LORD. (Proverbs 21:30)

God the Creator
The LORD by wisdom founded the earth;
  By understanding He established the heavens; (Proverbs 3:19)
By His knowledge the depths were broken up,
  And the clouds drop down the dew. (Proverbs 3:20)
By the *word* of the LORD were the heavens made;
  And all the hosts of them by the *breath* of His mouth. (Psalms 33:6)
The hearing ear and the seeing eye,
  The LORD has made them both. (Proverbs 20:12)
The LORD hath made all things for Himself:
  Yes, *even the wicked* for the day of evil! (Proverbs 16:4)

The Purposes of God
Ecclesiastes 3
[1] To everything there is a season,
  A time for every *purpose** under heaven:
[2] A time to be born, And a time to die;
  A time to plant, And a time to pluck what is planted;
[3] A time to kill, And a time to heal;
  A time to break down, And a time to build up;
[4] A time to weep, And a time to laugh;
  A time to mourn, And a time to dance;
[5] A time to cast away stones, And a time to gather stones;
  A time to embrace, And a time to refrain from embracing;
[6] A time to gain, And a time to lose;
  A time to keep, And a time to throw away;
[7] A time to tear, And a time to sew;
  A time to keep silence, And a time to speak;
[8] A time to love, And a time to hate;
  A time of war, And a time of peace.

*All of these things serve *God's* purposes!

The Ways of God
I know that, whatsoever God does, it shall be forever:
> Nothing can be put to it, nor any thing taken from it:
> **And God does it, that men should fear before Him!** (Ecclesiastes 3:14)

[God] has made everything beautiful in *His* time:
> Also He has set the world in [men's] heart,
> So that no man can find out the work that God makes
> From the beginning to the end. (Ecclesiastes 3:11)

...My thoughts are not your thoughts,
> Neither are your ways My ways, saith the LORD. (Isaiah 55:8)

For as the heavens are higher than the earth,
> So are My ways higher than your ways,
> And My thoughts [higher] than your thoughts. (Isaiah 55:9)

As thou knowest not what is the way of the spirit,
> Nor how the bones do grow in the womb of her that is with child:
> Even so thou knowest not the works of God
> Who maketh all. (Ecclesiastes 11:5)

I saw all the work of God,
> That a man cannot find out the work that is done under the sun.
> **For though a man labors to discover it, yet he will *not* find it;**
> **Moreover, though a wise man attempts to know it,**
> **He will *not* be able to find it!** (Ecclesiastes 8:17)

Trusting God in Adversity
..."What? shall we receive good at the hand of God,
> **And shall we not receive evil?"** (Job 2:10)

And [Job] said:
> ..."The LORD gave, and the LORD has taken away;
> **Blessed be the name of the LORD!"** (Job 1:21)

Consider the work of God: for who can make that straight,
> Which He has made crooked? (Ecclesiastes 7:13)

In the day of prosperity be joyful, but in the day of adversity consider:
> God also hath set the one over against the other,* *See: The Purposes of God - pg.9*
> To the end that man should find nothing
> After him (...that man does not know his future). (Ecclesiastes 7:14)

Say not thou, What is the cause that the former days
    Were better than these?
    For thou dost *not* enquire wisely concerning this. (Ecclesiastes 7:10)

In everything (all circumstances) **give thanks:**
    For *this* is the will of God
    In Christ Jesus concerning you! (1 Thessalonians 5:18)

The *fear* of man brings a snare:
    But whoso puts his trust in the LORD shall be safe. (Proverbs 29:25)

Trust in the LORD with all your heart,
    And lean not on your own understanding; (Proverbs 3:5)
In all your ways acknowledge Him,
    And He shall direct your paths! (Proverbs 3:6)

Do not be wise in your own eyes;
    Fear the LORD and depart from evil. (Proverbs 3:7)
It will be health to your flesh,
    And strength to your bones. (Proverbs 3:8)

He who heeds the word wisely will find good,
    And whoever trusts in the LORD, *happy* is he. (Proverbs 16:20)

The Word of God
Every word of God is pure;
    He is a shield to those who put their trust in Him. (Proverbs 30:5)
Do not add to His words,
    Lest He rebuke you, and you be found a liar. (Proverbs 30:6)

The Fear of the LORD

The fear of the LORD is to *hate* evil. (Proverbs 8:13)

The fear of the LORD is the beginning of wisdom,
    And the knowledge of the Holy One is understanding. (Proverbs 9:10)
The fear of the LORD is the beginning of knowledge,
    But fools *despise* wisdom and instruction. (Proverbs 1:7)
The fear of the LORD is a fountain of life,
    To turn one away from the snares of death. (Proverbs 14:27)
The fear of the LORD is the instruction of wisdom,
    And before honor is humility. (Proverbs 15:33)
By humility and the fear of the LORD
    Are riches and honor and life. (Proverbs 22:4)

In mercy and truth
    Atonement (redemption for mankind) is provided for iniquity;
    And by the fear of the LORD one *departs* from evil. (Proverbs 16:6)
The fear of the LORD is to *hate* evil;
    Pride and arrogance and the evil way
    And the perverse mouth I hate! (Proverbs 8:13)
He who walks in his uprightness fears the LORD,
    But he who *is* perverse in his ways *despises* Him. (Proverbs 14:2)

In the fear of the LORD there is strong confidence,
    And His children will have a place of refuge. (Proverbs 14:26)
The fear of the LORD prolongs days,
    But the years of the wicked will be shortened. (Proverbs 10:27)
The fear of the LORD leads to life,
    And he who has it will abide in satisfaction;
    He will not be visited with evil. (Proverbs 19:23)

Better is a little with the fear of the LORD,
    Than great treasure with trouble. (Proverbs 15:16)
Do not let your heart *envy* sinners,
    But be zealous (enthusiastic) for the fear of the LORD
    All the day; (Proverbs 23:17)
For surely there is a hereafter,
    And your hope will not be cut off. (Proverbs 23:18)

The Call to Wisdom, Knowledge & Understanding

...Wisdom exceeds folly
   As far as light exceeds darkness! (Ecclesiastes 2:13)
How much better to get wisdom than gold!
   And to get understanding is to be chosen
   Rather than silver! (Proverbs 16:16)

Proverbs 1
The Beginning of Knowledge
[1] The proverbs of Solomon the son of David, king of Israel:
[2] To know wisdom and instruction,
   To perceive (become aware of) the words of understanding,
[3] To receive the instruction of wisdom (being wise),
   Justice (what is right), judgment (the ability to make wise decisions),
   And equity (fairness and impartiality);
[4] To give prudence (exercising sound judgment in practical matters)
   To the simple (foolish),
[8] My son, hear the instruction of your father,
   And do not forsake the law of your mother;
[9] For they will be a graceful ornament on your head,
   And chains about your neck.

The Call of Wisdom
[20] Wisdom calls aloud outside;
   She raises her voice in the open squares.
[21] She cries out in the chief concourses (in the main streets),
   At the openings of the gates in the city
   She speaks her words:
[22] "How long, you simple ones, will you love simplicity?
   For scorners (those who loathe instruction)
   Delight in their scorning (contempt),
   And fools hate knowledge.
[23] Turn at my rebuke (reprimand);
   Surely I will pour out my spirit on you;
   I will make my words known to you.
[24] Because I have called and you refused,
   I have stretched out my hand and no one regarded,

²⁵ Because you disdained (thought it beneath you) all my counsel,
    And would have none of my rebuke,
²⁶ I also will *laugh* at your calamity (great misfortune);
    I will mock (make fun of you) when your terror comes,
²⁷ When your terror comes like a storm,
    And your destruction comes like a whirlwind,
    When distress (misery and suffering)
    And anguish (mental or physical pain) come upon you.
²⁸ Then they will call on me, but I will not answer;
    They will seek me diligently (with perseverance),
    But they will not find me.
²⁹ Because they hated knowledge
    And did not choose the fear of the LORD,
³⁰ They would have none of my counsel (advise)
    And despised my every rebuke.
³¹ Therefore they shall eat the fruit of their own way,
    And be filled to the full
    With their own fancies (that of which they are fond).
³² For the turning away of the simple will slay them,
    And the complacency (contentment or self-satisfaction)
    Of fools will destroy them;
³³ But whoever listens to me will dwell safely,
    And will be secure, without fear of evil."

Proverbs 2
The Value of Wisdom
¹ My son, if you receive my words,
    And treasure my commands within you,
² So that you incline your ear to wisdom,
    And apply your heart to understanding;
³ Yes, if you cry out for discernment (for good judgment),
    And lift up your voice for understanding,
⁴ If you seek her as silver,
    And search for her as for hidden treasures;
⁵ Then you will understand the fear of the LORD,
    And find the knowledge of God.
⁶ For the LORD gives wisdom;
    From His mouth come knowledge and understanding;

⁷ He stores up sound wisdom for the upright;
   He is a shield to those who walk uprightly;
⁸ He guards the paths of justice,
   And preserves the way of His saints.
⁹ Then you will understand righteousness and justice,
   Equity and every good path.
¹⁰ When wisdom enters your heart,
   And knowledge is *pleasant* to your soul,
¹¹ Discretion will preserve you;
   Understanding will keep you,
¹² [Wisdom will] deliver you from the way of evil,
   From the man who speaks
   Perverse things, (contrary to what is right and good)
¹³ From those who leave the paths of uprightness
   To walk in the ways of darkness;
¹⁴ Who rejoice in doing evil,
   And delight in the perversity of the wicked;
¹⁵ Whose ways are crooked,
   And who are devious (not straightforward) in their paths;
¹⁶ To deliver you from the immoral woman,
   From the seductress who flatters with her words,
¹⁷ Who forsakes the companion of her youth,
   And forgets the covenant of her God.
¹⁸ For her house leads down to death,
   And her paths to the dead;
¹⁹ **None who go to her return,**
   Nor do they regain the paths of life!
²⁰ So you may walk in the way of goodness,
   And keep to the paths of righteousness.
²¹ For the upright will dwell in the land,
   And the blameless will remain in it;
²² But the wicked will be cut off from the earth,
   And the unfaithful will be uprooted from it.

Proverbs 3
Guidance for the Young

[1] My son, do not forget my law,
    But let your heart keep my commands;
[2] For length of days and long life
    And peace they will add to you.
[3] Let not mercy and truth forsake you;
    Bind them around your neck,
    Write them on the tablet of your heart,
[4] And so find favor and high esteem
    In the sight of God *and* man.
[13] Happy is the man who finds wisdom,
    And the man who gains understanding;
[14] For her proceeds are better than the profits of silver,
    And her gain than fine gold.
[15] She is more precious than rubies,
    And *all* the things you may desire *cannot compare with her*!
[16] Length of days is in her right hand,
    In her left hand riches and honor.
[17] **Her ways are ways of *pleasantness*,**
    And all her paths are *peace*.
[18] She is a tree of life to those who take hold of her,
    And happy are all who retain (hold onto) her.
[21] My son, let them not depart from your eyes—
    Keep sound wisdom and discretion;
[22] So they will be life to your soul
    And grace to your neck.
[23] Then you will walk safely in your way,
    And your foot will not stumble.
[24] When you lie down, you will not be afraid;
    Yes, you will lie down and your sleep will be sweet.
[25] Do not be afraid of sudden terror,
    Nor of trouble from the wicked when it comes;
[26] For the LORD will be your confidence,
    And will keep your foot from being caught.

Proverbs 4
Security in Wisdom
[1] Hear, my children, the instruction of a father,
   And give attention to know understanding;
[2] For I give you good doctrine:
   Do not forsake my law!
[3] When I was my father's son,
   Tender and the only one in the sight of my mother,
[4] He also taught me, and said to me:
   "Let your heart retain my words;
   Keep my commands, and live.
[5] Get wisdom! Get understanding!
   Do not forget, nor turn away from the words of my mouth.
[6] Do not forsake her, and she will preserve you;
   Love her, and she will keep you.
[7] **Wisdom is the principal thing;**
   Therefore get wisdom.
   And in all your getting, get understanding!
[8] Exalt (praise) her, and she will promote you;
   She will bring you honor, when you embrace her.
[9] She will place on your head an ornament of grace;
   A crown of glory she will deliver to you."
[10] Hear, my son, and receive my sayings,
   And the years of your life will be many.
[11] I have taught you in the way of wisdom;
   I have led you in right paths.
[12] When you walk, your steps will not be hindered (filled with obstacles),
   And when you run, you will not stumble.
[13] Take firm hold of instruction, do not let go;
   Keep her, for she is your *life*!
[20] My son, give attention to my words;
   Incline your ear to my sayings.
[21] Do not let them depart from your eyes;
   Keep them in the midst of your heart;
[22] For they are life to those who find them,
   And health to all their flesh.
[23] Keep your heart with all diligence,
   For out of [the heart] spring the issues of life.
[24] Put away from you a deceitful (lying) mouth,
   And put perverse lips far from you.

[25] Let your eyes look straight ahead,
    And your eyelids look right before you.
[26] **Ponder** (consider very carefully) **the path of your feet,**
    And let all your ways be established.
[27] Do not turn to the right or the left;
    Remove your foot from evil.

Proverbs 6
The Light of Wisdom
[20] My son, keep your father's command,
    And do not forsake the law of your mother.
[21] Bind them *continually* upon your heart;
    Tie them around your neck.
[22] When you roam, they will lead you;
    When you sleep, they will keep you;
    And when you awake, they will speak with you.
[23] **For the commandment is a lamp,**
    And the law a light;
    Reproofs of instruction are the way of life!

[The word of God] is a lamp unto my feet
    And a light unto my path! (Psalms 119:105)

Proverbs 7
Treasure Wisdom
[1] My son, keep my words,
    And treasure my commands within you.
[2] Keep my commands and live,
    And my law as the apple of your eye.
[3] Bind them on your fingers;
    Write them on the tablet of your heart.
[4] Say to wisdom, "You are my sister,"
    And call understanding your nearest kin.

Proverbs 8
The Excellence of Wisdom

1 Does not wisdom cry out,
  And understanding lift up her voice?
2 She takes her stand on the top of the high hill,
  Beside the way, where the paths meet.
3 She cries out by the gates, at the entry of the city,
  At the entrance of the doors:
4 "To you, O men, I call,
  And my voice is to the sons of men.
5 O you simple ones, understand prudence (sound judgment),
  And you fools, be of an understanding heart.
6 Listen, for I will speak of excellent things,
  And from the opening of my lips will come right things;
7 For my mouth will speak truth;
  Wickedness is an abomination to my lips.
8 All the words of my mouth are with righteousness;
  Nothing crooked or perverse is in them.
9 They are all plain to him who understands,
  And right to those who find knowledge.
10 Receive my instruction, and not silver,
  And knowledge rather than choice gold;
11 For wisdom is better than rubies,
  And *all* the things one may desire *cannot* be compared with her!"
12 "I, wisdom, dwell with prudence,
  And find out knowledge and discretion.
13 **The fear of the LORD is to *hate* evil;**
  Pride and arrogance and the evil way
  And the perverse mouth I hate!
14 Counsel is mine, and sound wisdom;
  I am understanding, I have strength.
15 By me kings reign,
  And rulers decree justice.
16 By me princes rule, and nobles,
  All the judges of the earth.
17 I love those who love me,
  And those who seek me *diligently* will find me!
18 Riches and honor are with me,
  Enduring riches and righteousness.

¹⁹ My fruit is better than gold, yes, than fine gold,
  And my revenue than choice silver.
²⁰ I traverse (pass through) the way of righteousness,
  In the midst of the paths of justice,
²¹ That I may cause those who love me to inherit wealth,
  That I may fill their treasuries."
²² "The LORD possessed me at the beginning of His way,
  Before His works of old.
²³ I have been established from everlasting,
  From the beginning, before there was ever an earth.
²⁴ When there were no depths I was brought forth,
  When there were no fountains abounding with water.
²⁵ Before the mountains were settled,
  Before the hills, I was brought forth;
²⁶ While as yet He had not made the earth or the fields,
  Or the primal dust of the world.
²⁷ When He prepared the heavens, I was there,
  When He drew a circle on the face of the deep,
²⁸ When He established the clouds above,
  When He strengthened the fountains of the deep,
²⁹ When He assigned to the sea its limit,
  So that the waters would not transgress His command,
  When He marked out the foundations of the earth,
³⁰ Then I was beside Him as a master craftsman;
  And I was daily His delight,
  Rejoicing always before Him,
³¹ Rejoicing in His inhabited world,
  And my delight was with the sons of men."
³² "Now therefore, listen to me, my children,
  For blessed are those who keep my ways.
³³ Hear instruction and be wise,
  And do not disdain it (do not think it beneath you).
³⁴ *Blessed* is the man who listens to me,
  Watching daily at my gates,
  Waiting at the posts of my doors.
³⁵ **For whoever finds me finds life,**
  And obtains favor from the LORD!
³⁶ But he who sins against me wrongs his own soul;
  All those who hate me love death."

Proverbs 9
The Way of Wisdom
[1] Wisdom has built her house,
    She has hewn out her seven pillars;
[2] She has slaughtered her meat,
    She has mixed her wine,
    She has also furnished her table.
[3] She has sent out her maidens,
    She cries out from the highest places of the city,
[4] "Whoever is simple, let him turn in here!"
    As for him who lacks understanding, she says to him,
[5] "Come, eat of my bread
    And drink of the wine I have mixed.
[6] Forsake foolishness and live,
    And go in the way of understanding!"

Proverbs 19
The Value of Wisdom to the Soul
[2] Also it is not good for a soul to be without knowledge,
    And he sins who hastens with his feet.
[8] **He who gets wisdom loves his own soul**;
    He who keeps understanding will find good.
[16] He who keeps the commandment keeps his soul,
    But he who is careless of his ways will die.
[20] Listen to counsel and receive instruction,
    That you may be wise in your latter days.
[27] **Cease listening to instruction, my son,**
    And you *will* stray from the words of knowledge!

Proverbs 22
Sayings of the Wise
[17] Incline your ear and hear the words of the wise,
    And apply your heart to my knowledge;
[18] For it is a pleasant thing if you keep them within you;
    Let them all be fixed upon your lips,
[19] So that your trust may be in the LORD;
    I have instructed you today, even you.

[20] Have I not written to you excellent things
    Of counsels and knowledge,
[21] That I may make you know the certainty of the words of truth,
    That you may answer words of truth
    To those who send to you?

Proverbs 23
Give Your Heart to Wisdom
[12] Apply your heart to instruction,
    And your ears to words of knowledge.
[15] My son, if your heart is wise,
    My heart will rejoice—indeed, I myself;
[16] Yes, my inmost being will rejoice
    When your lips speak right things.
[22] Listen to your father who begot you,
    And do not despise your mother when she is old.
[23] **Buy the truth, and do not sell it,**
    Also wisdom and instruction and understanding.
[24] The father of the righteous will greatly rejoice,
    And he who begets a wise child will delight in him.
[25] Let your father and your mother be glad,
    And let her who bore you rejoice.
[26] My son, give me your heart,
    And let your eyes observe my ways!

Proverbs 24
The Sweetness of Wisdom
[13] My son, eat honey because it is good,
    And the honeycomb which is sweet to your taste;
[14] So shall the knowledge of wisdom be to your soul;
    If you have found it, there is a prospect (something expected),
    And your hope will not be cut off.

The Ultimate Wisdom!
...I [Solomon] gave my heart to seek and search out by wisdom
    Concerning all things that are done under heaven... (Ecclesiastes 1:13)
Let us hear the conclusion of the whole matter:
    Fear God and keep His commandments:
    For this is the whole duty of man. (Ecclesiastes 12:13)
For God shall bring every work into judgment,
    With every secret thing,
    Whether it be good, or whether it be evil. (Ecclesiastes 12:14)

If any of you lack wisdom, let him ask of God,
    That gives to *all men* liberally... (James 1:5)

Chastening and Correction

...Whom the LORD loves, He corrects. (Proverbs 3:12)

The Chastening of the LORD
My son, do not despise the chastening of the LORD,
    Nor detest His correction; (Proverbs 3:11)
For whom the LORD loves He corrects,
    Just as a father [corrects] the son in whom he delights. (Proverbs 3:12)

Correcting Children
Train up a child in the way he should go,
    And when he is old he will not depart from it. (Proverbs 22:6)
Correct your son, and he will give you rest;
    Yes, he will give delight to your soul. (Proverbs 29:17)
He who keeps instruction is in the way of life,
    But he who refuses correction *goes astray*. (Proverbs 10:17)
... He who hates correction is *stupid*! (Proverbs 12:1)
He who *despises* the word will be destroyed,
    But he who fears the commandment
    Will be rewarded. (Proverbs 13:13)

The Rod of Correction
Wisdom is found on the lips of him who has understanding,
    But a rod is for the back of him
    Who is devoid of understanding. (Proverbs 10:13)
The rod and rebuke give wisdom,
    But a child *left to himself*
    Brings *shame* to his mother! (Proverbs 29:15)
Foolishness is bound up in the heart of a child;
    The rod of correction will drive it far from him. (Proverbs 22:15)
He who spares his rod *hates* his son,
    But he who loves him disciplines him promptly. (Proverbs 13:24)
Do not withhold correction from a child,
    For if you beat him with a rod, he will not die. (Proverbs 23:13)
Chasten your son while there is hope,
    And do not let thy soul spare for his crying. (Proverbs 19:18) (KJV)

Blows that hurt cleanse away evil,
    As do stripes the inner depths of the heart. (Proverbs 20:30)
You shall beat him with a rod,
    And deliver his soul from hell. (Proverbs 23:14)
A whip for the horse,
    A bridle for the donkey,
    And a rod for the fool's back. (Proverbs 26:3)
He who is often rebuked, and hardens his neck,
    Will *suddenly* be destroyed, and that without remedy. (Proverbs 29:1)
Harsh discipline is for him who forsakes the way,
    And he who hates correction will die. (Proverbs 15:10)
Rebuke is more effective for a wise man
    Than a hundred blows on a fool. (Proverbs 17:10)
When the scoffer (mocker) is punished, the simple is made wise;
    But when the wise is instructed,
    He receives knowledge. (Proverbs 21:11)
Strike a scoffer (mocker), and the simple will become wary;
    Rebuke one who has understanding,
    And he will discern knowledge. (Proverbs 19:25)

A servant will not be corrected by mere words;
    For though he understands, he will not respond. (Proverbs 29:19)

The Wise Person

A wise man fears [the LORD] and departs from evil. (Proverbs 14:16)

The Wise Desire Instruction, Knowledge and Understanding
If you are wise, you are wise for yourself. (Proverbs 9:12)
A wise man will hear and increase learning,
    And a man of understanding will attain wise counsel, (Proverbs 1:5)
To understand a proverb and an enigma,
    The words of the wise and their riddles. (Proverbs 1:6)
The fear of the LORD is the beginning of knowledge,
    But fools *despise* wisdom and instruction. (Proverbs 1:7)
…He who wins souls is wise. (Proverbs 11:30)
The law of the wise is a fountain of life,
    To turn one away from the snares of death. (Proverbs 13:14)
The way of life winds upward for the wise,
    That he may turn away from hell below. (Proverbs 15:24)
Give instruction to a wise man, and he will be still wiser;
    Teach a just man, and he will increase in learning. (Proverbs 9:9)
A wise man fears [the LORD] and departs from evil, (Proverbs 14:16)
[And] the wise in heart will receive commands. (Proverbs 10:8)
The heart of the wise teaches his mouth,
    And adds learning to his lips. (Proverbs 16:23)
The highway of the upright is to depart from evil;
    He who keeps his way preserves his soul. (Proverbs 16:17)
[By wisdom] your days will be multiplied,
    And years of life will be added to you. (Proverbs 9:11)
The heart of the prudent (one with sound judgment) acquires knowledge,
    And the ear of the wise seeks knowledge. (Proverbs 18:15)
A scoffer (mocker) seeks wisdom and does not find it,
    But knowledge is easy to him who understands. (Proverbs 14:6)
Wise people store up knowledge, (Proverbs 10:14)
[And] a man of understanding has wisdom! (Proverbs 10:23)
Wisdom rests in the heart of him
    Who has understanding, (Proverbs 14:33)
[And] understanding is a wellspring of life
    To him who has it. (Proverbs 16:22)

A wise son *heeds* his father's instruction! (Proverbs 13:1)
Even a child is known by his deeds,
    Whether what he does is pure and right. (Proverbs 20:11)
Whoever loves instruction loves knowledge,
    But he who hates correction is *stupid*! (Proverbs 12:1)

The Favor of the Wise
The wise shall inherit glory, (Proverbs 3:35)
[And] among the upright there is favor. (Proverbs 14:9)
The crown of the wise is their riches; (Proverbs 14:24)
By knowledge the rooms are filled
    With all precious and pleasant riches. (Proverbs 24:4)
**...Whoever finds [wisdom] finds life,
    And obtains favor from the LORD!** (Proverbs 8:35)
Good understanding gains favor, (Proverbs 13:15)
[And] a man will be commended (praised)
    According to his wisdom. (Proverbs 12:8)
The king's favor is toward a wise servant, (Proverbs 14:35)
[And] a wise son makes a glad father; (Proverbs 10:1) (Proverbs 15:20)
Whoever loves wisdom makes his father rejoice! (Proverbs 29:3)
He who pampers his servant from childhood
    Will have him as a son in the end. (Proverbs 29:21)
A wise servant will rule over a son who causes shame,
    And will share an inheritance among the brothers. (Proverbs 17:2)
He who troubles his own house will inherit the wind,
    And the fool will be servant to the wise of heart. (Proverbs 11:29)
My son, be wise, and make my heart glad,
    That I may answer him who reproaches (accuses) me. (Proverbs 27:11)

The Strength of Wisdom
If you faint in the day of adversity,
    Your strength is small. (Proverbs 24:10)
A wise man is strong,
    Yes, a man of knowledge increases strength; (Proverbs 24:5)
Wisdom strengthens the wise
    More than ten mighty men which are in the city. (Ecclesiastes 7:19)
A wise man scales the city of the mighty,
    And brings down the trusted stronghold. (Proverbs 21:22)

Wisdom is better than strength;
>   Nevertheless, the poor man's wisdom is despised,
>   And his words are *not* heard. (Ecclesiastes 9:16)

...Wisdom is a defence, and money is a defence:
>   But the excellency of knowledge is, that wisdom gives life
>   To them that have it. (Ecclesiastes 7:12)

The Prudent Man
... He who receives correction is prudent, (Proverbs 15:5)
[And] the prudent (those with sound judgment)
>   [Are] crowned with knowledge. (Proverbs 14:18)

Every prudent man acts with knowledge, (Proverbs 13:16)
[And]... the prudent considers well his steps. (Proverbs 14:15)
Whoever keeps the law is a discerning son! (Proverbs 28:7)
Wisdom is in the sight of him who has understanding, (Proverbs 17:24)
[And] the wisdom of the prudent is to understand his way. (Proverbs 14:8)
The wise in heart will be called prudent,
>   And sweetness of the lips increases learning. (Proverbs 16:21)

A prudent man foresees evil and hides himself;
>   The simple pass on and are punished. (Proverbs 22:3) (Proverbs 27:12)

A prudent man (one who uses sound judgment)
>   Conceals knowledge, (Proverbs 12: 23)

[And] a prudent man covers shame. (Proverbs 12:16)

The Wise Man Heeds Counsel
...He who heeds counsel is wise. (Proverbs 12:15)
Without counsel, plans go awry:
>   But In the multitude of counselors
>   [Plans] are established. (Proverbs 15:22)

Plans are established by counsel;
>   By wise counsel wage war. (Proverbs 20:18)

...By wise counsel you will wage your own war,
>   And in a multitude of counselors there is safety. (Proverbs 24:6)

Where there is no counsel, the people fall;
>   But in the multitude of counselors there is safety. (Proverbs 11:14)

The horse is prepared for the day of battle,
>   But deliverance is of the *LORD*! (Proverbs 21:31)

Rebuking the Wise
These things also belong to the wise:
    It is not good to show partiality (favoritism)
    In judgment. (Proverbs 24:23)
He who says to the wicked, "You are righteous,"
    Him the people will curse;
    Nations will abhor (hate) him. (Proverbs 24:24)
But those who rebuke the wicked will have delight,
    And a good blessing will come upon them. (Proverbs 24:25)
Open rebuke is better
    Than love carefully concealed. (Proverbs 27:5)
He who rebukes a man will find more favor afterward
    Than he who flatters with the tongue. (Proverbs 28:23)
Like an earring of gold and an ornament of fine gold
    Is a wise rebuker to an obedient ear. (Proverbs 25:12)
Faithful are the wounds of a friend; (Proverbs 27:6)
The ear that hears the rebukes of life
    Will abide among the wise. (Proverbs 15:31)
He who disdains instruction (thinks it beneath him) despises his own soul,
    But he who heeds rebuke gets understanding. (Proverbs 15:32)
... **He who regards a rebuke will be honored!** (Proverbs 13:18)

*See also: The Mouth of the Wise and Foolish - pg. 64
    The Wise and Foolish Hearts - pg. 75

The Foolish Person

The *fool* has said in his heart "there is no God"! (Psalms 14:1)

The Foolish Despise Wisdom, Knowledge and Understanding
A fool despises his father's instruction, (Proverbs 15:5)
[And] a foolish man despises his mother. (Proverbs 15:20)
Wisdom is in the sight of him who has understanding,
    But the eyes of a fool
        Are on the ends of the earth. (Proverbs 17:24)
Wisdom is too lofty for a fool;
    He does not open his mouth
        In the gate [where wisdom calls]. (Proverbs 24:7)
...He who sins against [wisdom] wrongs his own soul;
    All those who hate [wisdom] love death. (Proverbs 8:36)
...Fools die for lack of wisdom. (Proverbs 10:21)
...He who follows frivolity (light-minded things)
    Is devoid of understanding, (Proverbs 12:11)
[And] a man who wanders from the way of understanding
    Will rest in the assembly of the dead. (Proverbs 21:16)
[Wisdom], Deliver those who are drawn toward death,
    And hold back those stumbling to the slaughter. (Proverbs 24:11)

Fools Delight in Sin
Fools mock at sin, (Proverbs 14:9)
[And] to do evil is like sport to a fool. (Proverbs 10:23)
*Folly is *joyous* to him
    Who is destitute of (lacks) **wisdom,** (Proverbs 15:21) (KJV)
[And]...it is an abomination to fools to depart from evil! (Proverbs 13:19)
...The foolishness of fools is folly (foolish actions), (Proverbs 14:24)
*[And] the folly (foolish actions) **of fools**
    Is *deceit* (is what deceives others)**!** (Proverbs 14:8)
*Be doers of the Word, and not hearers only
    Deceiving your own selves! (James 1:22)
The foolishness of a man twists his way,
    And his heart *frets* against (is angry with) **the LORD!** (Proverbs 19:3)
The devising of foolishness is sin,
    And the scoffer (mocker) is an abomination to men. (Proverbs 24:9)
... If you scoff, you will bear it alone. (Proverbs 9:12)

A Fool Does Not See His Sin
Most men will proclaim each his own goodness,
   But who can find a faithful man? (Proverbs 20:6)
Who can say, "I have made my heart clean,
   I am pure from my sin"? (Proverbs 20:9)
The way of a fool is right *in his own eyes*! (Proverbs 12: 15)

The Foolish Lack Self-Control
A fool's wrath is known at once; (Proverbs 12: 16)
A fool's lips enter into contention (disputes),
   And his mouth calls for blows (fighting). (Proverbs 18:6)
A quick-tempered man acts foolishly, (Proverbs 14: 17)
[And] he who is impulsive *exalts* (praises) folly. (Proverbs 14:29)
Whoever has no rule over his own spirit
   Is like a city broken down, without walls. (Proverbs 25:28)
Let a man meet a bear robbed of her cubs,
   Rather than a fool in his folly. (Proverbs 17:12)
...A fool rages and is self-confident; (Proverbs 14:16)
Do you see a man hasty in his words?
   There is more hope for a fool than for him! (Proverbs 29:20)
In the multitude of words sin is *not* lacking! (Proverbs 10:19)

Contending with the Foolish
If a wise man contends with a foolish man,
   Whether the fool *rages* or *laughs*, there is no peace. (Proverbs 29:9)
Like a madman who throws
   Firebrands, arrows, and death, (Proverbs 26:18)
Is the man who deceives his neighbor,
   And says, "I was only joking!" (Proverbs 26:19)

The Shame of Foolishness
The simple inherit folly (foolish actions), (Proverbs 14:18)
And *shame* shall be the legacy (what is remembered)
   Of fools! (Proverbs 3:35)
As snow in summer and rain in harvest,
   So honor is *not* fitting for a fool. (Proverbs 26:1)
Like one who binds a stone in a sling
   Is he who gives honor to a fool. (Proverbs 26:8)

...A companion of gluttons shames his father, (Proverbs 28:7)
And the companion of fools will be destroyed. (Proverbs 13:20)
[The king's] wrath is against him who causes shame. (Proverbs 14:35)

The Sorrow of a Fool's Parents
He who begets a scoffer does so to his sorrow,
    And the father of a fool has no joy. (Proverbs 17:21)
A foolish son is a grief to his father,
    And bitterness to her who bore him. (Proverbs 17:25)
...A foolish son is the *grief* of his mother, (Proverbs 10:1)
[And] a foolish son is the *ruin* of his father. (Proverbs 19:13)
He who mistreats his father and chases away his mother
    Is a son who causes shame
    And brings reproach (disgrace). (Proverbs 19:26)

The Correction of Fools
...The way of the unfaithful is hard, (Proverbs 13:15)
But the correction of fools is *folly* (a foolish action). (Proverbs 16:22)
Do not speak in the hearing of a fool,
    For he will despise (loathe) the wisdom of your words; (Proverbs 23:9)
... Fools despise wisdom and instruction, (Proverbs 1:7)
[And]...a scoffer (mocker) does not listen to rebuke. (Proverbs 13:1)
A man who isolates himself seeks his own desire;
    He rages against all wise judgment. (Proverbs 18:1)
Do not answer a fool according to his folly,
    Lest you also be like him. (Proverbs 26:4)
Answer a fool according to his folly,
    Lest he be wise in his own eyes. (Proverbs 26:5)
Do you see a man *wise in his own eyes*?
    There is more hope for a fool than for him! (Proverbs 26:12)
Poverty *and* shame will come to him
    Who disdains correction (thinks it beneath him). (Proverbs 13:18)
Though you grind a fool in a mortar
    With a pestle along with crushed grain,
    Yet his foolishness will not depart from him. (Proverbs 27:22)

*See also: The Mouth of the Wise and Foolish - pg. 64
    The Wise and Foolish Hearts - pg. 75

The Righteous Person

In the way of righteousness is life
   And in its pathway there is no death. (Proverbs 12:28)

The LORD Blesses the Righteous
The eyes of the LORD are in every place,
   Keeping watch on the evil and the good. (Proverbs 15:3)
To do righteousness and justice
   Is more acceptable to the LORD than sacrifice. (Proverbs 21:3)
Blessings are on the head of the righteous, (Proverbs 10:6)
[And the LORD] blesses the home of the just. (Proverbs 3:33)
…The tent of the upright will flourish, (Proverbs 14:11)
[And] the house of the righteous will stand. (Proverbs 12:7)
The light of the righteous rejoices; (Proverbs 13:9)
… The righteous sings and rejoices. (Proverbs 29:6)
When the righteous rejoice, there is great glory; (Proverbs 28:12)
When it goes well with the righteous, the city rejoices. (Proverbs 11:10)
By the blessing of the upright the city is exalted, (Proverbs 11:11)
[And] righteousness *exalts* (prospers) a nation! (Proverbs 14:34)

God Hears the Prayers of the Righteous
The desire of the righteous is only good. (Proverbs 11:23)
He who earnestly seeks good finds favor; (Proverbs 11:27)
A good man obtains favor from the LORD (Proverbs 12:2)
[And] a good man will be satisfied from above. (Proverbs 14:14)
…To the righteous, good shall be repaid. (Proverbs 13:21)
The hope of the righteous will be gladness, (Proverbs 10:28)
[And] the blameless will inherit good. (Proverbs 28:10)
…**The desire of the righteous will be granted,** (Proverbs 10:24)
[And] happy is he who keeps the law! (Proverbs 29:18)
[The LORD] hears the prayer of the righteous! (Proverbs 15:29)
… Jabez was *more honorable* than his brethren:
   And his mother called his name Jabez, saying,
      Because I bare him with sorrow. (I Chronicles 4:9)

And Jabez called on the God of Israel, saying,
> Oh that thou would bless me indeed, and enlarge my coast,
> And that thy hand might be with me,
> And that thou would keep me from evil, that it may not grieve me!
> And God granted him that which he requested. (I Chronicles 4:10)

Deliverance of the Righteous
...Righteousness leads to life! (Proverbs 11:19)
In the way of righteousness is life
> And in its pathway there is no death. (Proverbs 12:28)

The way of the LORD is *strength* for the upright, (Proverbs 10:29)
[And] as for the upright, [the LORD] establishes his way. (Proverbs 21:29)
...Through knowledge the righteous will be delivered. (Proverbs 11:9)
The righteousness of the upright will deliver them (Proverbs 11:6)
[For]...righteousness delivers from death. (Proverbs 10:2)
Whoever walks blamelessly will be saved. (Proverbs 28:18)
The bloodthirsty *hate* the blameless,
> But the upright seek his soul. (Proverbs 29:10) (KJV)

An unjust man is an *abomination* to the righteous,
> **And he who is upright in the way**
> **Is an *abomination* to the wicked!** (Proverbs 29:27)

Thorns and snares are in the way of the perverse;
> [But] he who guards his soul will be far from them. (Proverbs 22:5)

No grave trouble will overtake the righteous; (Proverbs 12:21)
....The righteous will come through trouble, (Proverbs 12:13)
[And]... see [the fall of the wicked]. (Proverbs 29:16)

The Root of the Righteous
...The root of the righteous yields fruit, (Proverbs 12:12)
[And]... the root of the righteous cannot be moved. (Proverbs 12:3)
The righteous will never be removed (Proverbs 10:30)
[For]...the righteous has an everlasting foundation. (Proverbs 10:25)

The Honor and Integrity of the Righteous
A man's steps are of the LORD;
> How then can a man understand his own way? (Proverbs 20:24)

The righteous man walks in his integrity; (Proverbs 20:7)

... The path of the just is like the shining sun,
    That shines ever brighter unto the perfect day. (Proverbs 4:18)
He who walks with integrity walks securely. (Proverbs 10:9)
The righteousness of the blameless
    Will direct his way aright, (Proverbs 11:5)
[And] the integrity of the upright will guide them. (Proverbs 11:3)
He who follows righteousness and mercy
    Finds life, righteousness, and honor. (Proverbs 21:21)
...The righteous are bold as a lion, (Proverbs 28:1)
[And] righteousness guards him whose way is blameless. (Proverbs 13:6)
... The blameless in their ways are [the LORD's] delight. (Proverbs 11:20)
Those who forsake the law *praise* the wicked,
    But such as keep the law
    Contend (disputes) with them. (Proverbs 28:4)

The Thoughts of the Righteous
Commit your works to the LORD,
    And your thoughts will be established! (Proverbs 16:3)
The thoughts of the righteous are right, (Proverbs 12:5)
[And] it is a joy for the just to do justice. (Proverbs 21:15)
The righteous considers the cause of the poor, (Proverbs 29:7)
[And]...regards the life of his animal. (Proverbs 12:10)

The Labor of the Righteous
The person who labors, labors for himself,
    For his hungry mouth drives him on. (Proverbs 16:26)
The labor of the righteous leads to life, (Proverbs 10:16)
And the recompense of a man's hands
    Will be rendered to him. (Proverbs 12:14)
...As for the pure, his work is right. (Proverbs 21:8)
The LORD will not allow the righteous soul to famish. (Proverbs 10:3)
The wicked man does deceptive work;
    But he who sows righteousness
    Will have a sure reward. (Proverbs 11:18)
The righteous eats to the satisfying of his soul. (Proverbs 13:25)
A satisfied soul loathes the honeycomb,
    But to a hungry soul...every bitter thing is sweet. (Proverbs 27:7)

The Glory of the Righteous
The glory of young men is their strength,
    And the splendor of old men is their gray head. (Proverbs 20:29)
The silver-haired head is a crown of glory,
    If it is found in the way of righteousness. (Proverbs 16:31)
Children's children are the crown of old men,
    And the glory of children is their father; (Proverbs 17:6)
His children are blessed after him. (Proverbs 20:7)
A good man leaves an inheritance
    To his children's children, (Proverbs 13:22)
[And] the posterity (future generations) of the righteous
    Will be delivered. (Proverbs 11:21)
...The righteous has a refuge in his death (Proverbs 14:32)
[For]...the memory of the righteous is blessed. (Proverbs 10:7)

Sins of the Righteous
A righteous man who falters before the wicked
    Is like a murky spring and a polluted well! (Proverbs 25: 26)

Dead flies cause the ointment of the apothecary
    To send forth a stinking savor:
    So doth a little folly him that is in reputation
    For wisdom and honor! (Ecclesiastes 10:1)

Wisdom is better than weapons of war:
    But one sinner destroys much good! (Ecclesiastes 9:18)

*See also: The Mouth of the Righteous - pg. 65
*The Righteous Man does not follow his heart. He follows God's commands!

The Wicked Person

Whoever rewards evil for good,
    Evil *will not* depart from his house! (Proverbs 17:13)

The Destruction of the Wicked
The eyes of the LORD are in every place,
    Keeping watch on the evil and the good. (Proverbs 15:3)
A man is *not* established by wickedness, (Proverbs 12:3)
[And] sin is a *reproach* (disgrace) **to *any* people!** (Proverbs 14:34)
It is not good to show partiality (favoritism) to the wicked,
    Or to overthrow the righteous in judgment. (Proverbs 18:5)
If the righteous will be recompensed (rewarded) on the earth,
    How much more the ungodly and the sinner. (Proverbs 11:31)
The LORD is far from the wicked, (Proverbs 15:29)
[And] surely He scorns (loathes) the scornful. (Proverbs 3:34)
…The expectation of the wicked is [the LORD's] wrath. (Proverbs 11:23)
The righteous is delivered from trouble,
    And it comes to the wicked instead. (Proverbs 11:8)
Evil pursues sinners, (Proverbs 13:21)
[And] trouble will come to him who seeks evil. (Proverbs 11:27)
…Wickedness overthrows the sinner; (Proverbs 13:6)
A man of wicked intentions [the LORD] will condemn. (Proverbs 12:2)
An evil man seeks only rebellion;
    Therefore a cruel messenger will be sent against him. (Proverbs 17:11)
… He who pursues evil pursues it to his own death. (Proverbs 11:19)
A man who wanders from the way of understanding
    Will rest in the assembly of the dead. (Proverbs 21:16)
The fear of the wicked will come upon him, (Proverbs 10:24)
[And] he who is perverse in his ways will suddenly fall! (Proverbs 28:18)
…**His calamity** (great misfortune) **shall come suddenly;**
    Suddenly he shall be broken *without remedy*! (Proverbs 6:15)
When the whirlwind passes by, the wicked is no more, (Proverbs 10:25)
[And] the house of the wicked will be overthrown. (Proverbs 14:11)
The righteous God wisely considers the house of the wicked,
    Overthrowing the wicked for their wickedness. (Proverbs 21:12)
The curse of the LORD is on the house of the wicked, (Proverbs 3:33)
[And] destruction will come to the workers
    Of iniquity (wickedness). (Proverbs 10:29) (Proverbs 21:15)

...[The city] is overthrown by the mouth of the wicked. (Proverbs 11:11)
Like a flitting sparrow, like a flying swallow,
    So a curse without cause shall not alight. (Proverbs 26:2)
When the wicked are multiplied,
    Transgression (sin) increases; (Proverbs 29:16)
...When the wicked arise,
    Men hide themselves. (Proverbs 28:12) (Proverbs 28:28)
Do not fret (worry) because of evildoers,
    Nor be envious of the wicked; (Proverbs 24:19)
Though they join forces,
    The wicked *will not* go unpunished. (Proverbs 11:21)
...There will be no prospect for the evil man; (Proverbs 24:20)
By transgression (sin), an evil man is snared. (Proverbs 29:6)
Do they not go astray who devise evil?
    But mercy and truth belong
    To those who devise good. (Proverbs 14:22)
He who sows iniquity will reap *sorrow*,
    And the rod of his anger will fail. (Proverbs 22:8)
...The wicked will fall by his own wickedness; (Proverbs 11:5)
...The unfaithful will be caught by their lust, (Proverbs 11:6)
[And] the wicked shall be filled with evil. (Proverbs 12:21)
The perversity of the unfaithful will *destroy* them! (Proverbs 11:3)
The violence of the wicked will destroy them,
    Because they refuse to do justice. (Proverbs 21:7)
Evil men do not understand justice,
    But those who seek the LORD understand all. (Proverbs 28:5)
The lamp of the wicked will be put out, (Proverbs 24:20) (Proverbs 13:9)
[And] the righteous will see their fall. (Proverbs 29:16)
The wicked shall be a ransom for the righteous,
    And the unfaithful [a ransom] for the upright. (Proverbs 21:18)
The wicked is banished in his wickedness, (Proverbs 14:32)
[And] the wicked will not inhabit the earth. (Proverbs 10:30)
The wicked are overthrown and are no more. (Proverbs 12:7)
The evil will bow before the good,
    And the wicked [will bow]
    At the gates of the righteous. (Proverbs 14:19)
An unjust man is an abomination to the righteous, (Proverbs 29:27)
[And] the name of the wicked will rot. (Proverbs 10:7)
...When the wicked perish, there is jubilation. (Proverbs 11:10)

Notable Characteristics of the Wicked
A wicked man hardens his face; (Proverbs 21:29)
He winks with his eyes,
    He shuffles his feet,
    He points with his fingers. (Proverbs 6:13)
He who winks with the eye causes trouble; (Proverbs 10:10)
He winks his eye to devise perverse things.
    He moves his lips and brings about evil. (Proverbs 16:30) (KJV)
He devises evil continually. (Proverbs 6:14)

The Path of the Wicked
Do not be *envious* of evil men,
    Nor desire to be with them; (Proverbs 24:1)
Do not enter the path of the wicked,
    And do not walk in the way of evil. (Proverbs 4:14)
Avoid it, do not travel on it;
    Turn away from it and pass on. (Proverbs 4:15)
For they do not sleep unless they have done evil;
    And their sleep is taken away
    Unless they make someone fall. (Proverbs 4:16)
For they eat the bread of wickedness,
    And drink the wine of violence. (Proverbs 4:17)
A violent man entices his neighbor,
    And leads him in a way that is not good. (Proverbs 16:29)
Whoever causes the upright to go astray in an evil way,
    He himself will fall into his own pit. (Proverbs 28:10)
He that digs a pit shall fall into it; and whoso breaks a hedge,
    A serpent shall bite him. (Ecclesiastes 10:8)
Thorns and snares are in the way of the perverse. (Proverbs 22:5)
The way of the wicked is like darkness;
    They do not know what makes them stumble. (Proverbs 4:19)

The Wicked are Pure in Their Own Eyes
There is a generation that is pure in its own eyes,
    Yet is not washed from its filthiness. (Proverbs 30:12)
There is a generation—oh, how lofty are their eyes!
    And their eyelids are lifted up. (Proverbs 30:13)
Every way of a man is right *in his own eyes*,
    But the LORD weighs the hearts. (Proverbs 21:2)
All the ways of a man are pure *in his own eyes*,
    But the LORD weighs the spirits. (Proverbs 16:2)
There is a way that seems right to a man,
    But its end is the way of death. (Proverbs 14:12) (Proverbs 16:25)
If you say, "Surely we did not know this,"
    Does not *He* who weighs the hearts consider it?
    He who keeps your soul, does *He* not know it?
    And will *He* not render to each man
    According to his deeds? (Proverbs 24:12)

The Guilty Man
The way of a guilty man is perverse; (Proverbs 21:8)
The wicked flee when no one pursues! (Proverbs 28:1)
A man burdened with bloodshed will flee into a pit;
    Let no one help him. (Proverbs 28:17)

Shame of the Wicked
When the wicked comes, contempt comes also; (Proverbs 18:3)
…A wicked man is loathsome and comes to shame. (Proverbs 13:5)
…With dishonor comes reproach (disgrace), (Proverbs 18:3)
And a man of wicked intentions is hated. (Proverbs 14:17)
…The expectation of the wicked will perish. (Proverbs 10:28)
When a wicked man dies, his expectation will perish,
    And the hope of the unjust perishes. (Proverbs 11:7)

*See also: The Mouth of the Wicked - pg. 66
    The Heart of the Wicked - pg. 75

The Proud Person

Do not boast about tomorrow,
    For you do not know what a day may bring forth! (Proverbs 27:1)

In the mouth of a fool is a rod of pride,
    But the lips of the wise will preserve them. (Proverbs 14:3)
When pride comes, then comes shame;
    But with the humble is wisdom. (Proverbs 11:2)
Better to be of a humble spirit with the lowly,
    Than to divide the spoil with the proud. (Proverbs 16:19)
A man's pride will bring him low,
    But the humble in spirit will retain honor! (Proverbs 29:23)

Before destruction the heart of a man is haughty (arrogant),
    And before honor is humility. (Proverbs 18:12)
The LORD will *destroy* the house of the proud,
    But He will establish the boundary of the widow. (Proverbs 15:25)
Everyone proud in heart is an abomination to the LORD;
    Though they join forces, *none* will go unpunished. (Proverbs 16:5)
Surely [the LORD] scorns (loathes) the scornful,
    But gives grace to the humble. (Proverbs 3:34)

Pride goes before destruction,
    And a haughty (arrogant) spirit before a fall. (Proverbs 16:18)
A haughty look, a proud heart,
    And the plowing of the wicked are sin. (Proverbs 21:4)
A proud and haughty man—"Scoffer" (mocker) **is his name;**
    He acts with arrogant pride. (Proverbs 21:24)
By pride comes nothing but *strife*,
    But with the well-advised is wisdom. (Proverbs 13:10)
He who is of a proud heart stirs up strife (quarrels),
    But he who trusts in the LORD will be prospered. (Proverbs 28:25)
Cast out the scoffer (mocker), and contention (disputes) will leave;
    Yes, strife (quarrels) and reproach (accusations)
    will cease. (Proverbs 22:10)

He who corrects a scoffer (mocker) ***gets shame for himself*,**
     And he who rebukes a wicked man
     ***Only harms himself*!** (Proverbs 9:7)
Do not correct a scoffer, lest he hate you;
     Rebuke a wise man, and he will love you. (Proverbs 9:8)
A scoffer does not love one who corrects him,
     Nor will he go to the wise. (Proverbs 15:12)
The devising (planning) of foolishness is sin,
     And the scoffer is an abomination to men. (Proverbs 24:9)
He who begets a scoffer does so to his sorrow,
     And the father of a fool has no joy. (Proverbs 17:21)
Judgments are prepared for scoffers,
     And beatings for the backs of fools. (Proverbs 19:29)

Abominations

An unjust man is an *abomination* to the righteous,
**   And he who is upright in the way**
Is an *abomination* to the wicked. (Proverbs 29:27)

These six things the LORD hates,
    Yes, seven are an abomination to Him: (Proverbs 6:16)
A proud look,
    A lying tongue,
    Hands that shed innocent blood, (Proverbs 6:17)
A heart that devises wicked plans,
    Feet that are swift in running to evil, (Proverbs 6:18)
A false witness who speaks lies,
    And one who sows discord among brethren. (Proverbs 6:19)

Lying lips are an abomination to the LORD,
    But those who deal truthfully are His delight. (Proverbs 12:22)
Diverse (purposefully inaccurate) weights and diverse measures,
    They are both alike, an abomination to the LORD. (Proverbs 20:10)
Diverse weights are an abomination to the LORD,
    And dishonest scales are not good. (Proverbs 20:23)
Dishonest scales are an abomination to the LORD,
    But a just weight is His delight. (Proverbs 11:1)

The way of the wicked is an abomination to the LORD,
    But He loves him who follows righteousness. (Proverbs 15:9)
It is an abomination for kings to commit wickedness,
    For a throne is established by righteousness. (Proverbs 16:12)
The thoughts of the wicked are an abomination to the LORD,
    But the words of the pure are pleasant. (Proverbs 15:26)
Those who are of a perverse heart are an abomination to the LORD,
    But the blameless in their ways are His delight. (Proverbs 11:20)
One who turns away his ear from hearing the law,
    ***Even his prayer* is an abomination!** (Proverbs 28:9)
The sacrifice of the wicked is an abomination to the LORD,
    But the prayer of the upright is His delight. (Proverbs 15:8)

The sacrifice of the wicked is an abomination;
    How much more when he brings it
    With wicked intent! (Proverbs 21:27)

He who justifies the wicked, and he who condemns the just,
    ***Both* of them alike are an abomination to the LORD**. (Proverbs 17:15)
Everyone proud in heart is an abomination to the LORD;
    Though they join forces, none will go unpunished. (Proverbs 16:5)

Riches and Poverty

He that loves silver shall *not* be satisfied with silver;
    Nor he that loves abundance with increase! (Ecclesiastes 5:10)

Not Too Rich, Not Too Poor
Two things I request of You
    (Deprive me not before I die): (Proverbs 30:7)
Remove falsehood and lies far from me;
    Give me neither poverty nor riches—
    Feed me with the food allotted to me; (Proverbs 30:8)
Lest I be full and deny You,
    And say, "Who is the LORD?"
    Or lest I be poor and steal,
    And profane (disrespect) the [sacred] name of my God. (Proverbs 30:9)

Diligence to Obtain Wealth
He who has a slack hand becomes poor,
    But the hand of the *diligent* (hard-working) makes rich. (Proverbs 10:4)
He that observes the wind shall not sow;
    And he that regards the clouds shall not reap. (Ecclesiastes 11:4)
Where no oxen are, the trough is clean;
    But much increase comes by the strength of an ox. (Proverbs 14:4)
Prepare your outside work,
    Make it fit for yourself in the field;
    And afterward build your house. (Proverbs 24:27)
Be diligent to know the state of your flocks,
    And attend to your herds; (Proverbs 27:23)
For riches *are not* forever,
    Nor does a crown endure to all generations. (Proverbs 27:24)
When the hay is removed, and the tender grass shows itself,
    And the herbs of the mountains are gathered in, (Proverbs 27:25)
The lambs will provide your clothing,
    And the goats the price of a field; (Proverbs 27:26)
You shall have enough goats' milk for your food,
    For the food of your household,
    And the nourishment of your maidservants. (Proverbs 27:27)

False Confidence in Riches

The name of the LORD is a strong tower;
>The righteous run to it and are safe. (Proverbs 18:10)

The rich man's wealth is *his* strong city,
>**And like a high wall in his own esteem!** (Proverbs 18:11)

The rich man is wise *in his own eyes*,
>But the poor who has understanding
>Searches Him out. (Proverbs 28:11)

The rich man's wealth is his strong city;
>**The destruction of the poor is *their poverty*!** (Proverbs 10:15)

The poor you will *always* have with you! (Matthew 26:11)

Do not overwork to be rich;
>**Because of your own understanding...cease!** (Proverbs 23:4)

Will you set your eyes on that which is not?
>**For riches certainly make themselves wings;**
>**They fly away like an eagle toward heaven!** (Proverbs 23:5)

He who trusts in his riches *will fall*,
>But the righteous will flourish like foliage. (Proverbs 11:28)

Riches do not profit in the day of wrath,
>But righteousness delivers from death. (Proverbs 11:4)

The ransom of a man's life is his riches,
>But the poor does not hear rebuke. (Proverbs 13:8)

The *blessing of the LORD* makes one rich,
>And He adds *no* sorrow with it. (Proverbs 10:22)

Go to now, you that say, Today or tomorrow we will go into such a city,
>And continue there a year, and buy and sell, and get gain: (James 4:13)

Whereas you know not what shall be on the morrow.
>For what is your life?
>It is even a vapor, that appears for a little time,
>And then vanishes away. (James 4:14)

For that you ought to say,
>*If the LORD will*, we shall live, and do this, or that. (James 4:15)

The great God who formed everything
>Gives the fool his hire and the transgressor his wages. (Proverbs 26:10)

Every man also to whom God hath given riches and wealth,
>**And hath given him power to eat thereof, and to take his portion,**
>**And to rejoice in his labor; this is the *gift* of God!** (Ecclesiastes 5:19)

For he shall not much remember the days of his life;
>Because God answers him in the *joy* of his heart. (Ecclesiastes 5:20)

In the day of prosperity be joyful, but in the day of adversity consider:
    God also hath set the one over against the other,
    To the end that man should find nothing after him. (Ecclesiastes 7:14)
...The race is not to the swift, nor the battle to the strong,
    Neither yet bread to the wise, nor yet riches to men of understanding,
    Nor yet favor to men of skill;
    But *time* and *chance* happens to them all! (Ecclesiastes 9:11)

Contentment
He that loves silver shall *not* be satisfied with silver;
    Nor he that loves abundance with increase! (Ecclesiastes 5:10)
The sleep of a laboring man is sweet, whether he eats little or much:
    But the abundance of the rich
    Will not suffer him to sleep. (Ecclesiastes 5:12)
Better is a handful with quietness,
    Than both hands full with travail
    And vexation of spirit! (Ecclesiastes 4:6)
Better is a little with righteousness,
    Than vast revenues without justice. (Proverbs 16:8)
Better is a dry morsel with quietness,
    Than a house full of feasting with strife. (Proverbs 17:1)
Better is a dinner of herbs where love is,
    Than a fatted calf with hatred. (Proverbs 15:17)

Say not thou,
    What is the cause that the former days were better than these?
    For thou dost *not* enquire wisely concerning this. (Ecclesiastes 7:10)

Wealth Makes Many Friends
Wealth makes *many* friends,
    But the poor is separated from his friend. (Proverbs 19:4)
The poor man is hated even by his own neighbor,
    But the rich has many friends. (Proverbs 14:20)
The poor man uses entreaties,
    But the rich answers *roughly*. (Proverbs 18:23)
All the brothers of the poor hate him;
    How much more do his friends go far from him!
    He may pursue them with words,
    Yet they abandon him. (Proverbs 19:7)

Giving
Honor the LORD with your possessions,
>And with the first-fruits of all your increase; (Proverbs 3:9)

So your barns will be filled with plenty,
>And your vats will overflow with new wine. (Proverbs 3:10)

There is one who makes himself rich, yet has nothing;
>And one who makes himself poor, yet has great riches. (Proverbs 13:7)

There is one who scatters, yet increases more;
>And there is one who withholds more than is right,
>But it leads to poverty. (Proverbs 11:24)

The generous soul *will* be made rich,
>And he who waters will also be watered himself. (Proverbs 11:25)

He who has a generous eye will be blessed,
>For he gives of his bread to the poor. (Proverbs 22:9)

Cast thy bread upon the waters:
>For thou shalt find it after many days. (Ecclesiastes 11:1)

Give a portion to seven, and also to eight; For thou knowest not
>What evil shall be upon the earth. (Ecclesiastes 11:2)

…The profit of the earth is for all:
>The king himself is served by the field. (Ecclesiastes 5:9)

The people will *curse* him who withholds grain,
>But blessing will be on the head of him who sells it. (Proverbs 11:26)

He who gives to the poor will not lack,
>But he who hides his eyes will have *many* curses. (Proverbs 28:27)

Much food is in the fallow ground of the poor,
>And for lack of justice there is waste. (Proverbs 13:23)

Considering the Poor
He who despises his neighbor sins;
>But he who has mercy on the poor, happy is he. (Proverbs 14:21)

The merciful man does good for his own soul,
>But he who is cruel troubles his own flesh. (Proverbs 11:17)

The righteous considers the cause of the poor,
>But the wicked does not understand such knowledge. (Proverbs 29:7)

He who has pity on the poor lends to the LORD,
>And [the LORD] will pay back what he has given. (Proverbs 19:17)

The lips of the righteous feed many; (Proverbs 10:21)

Whoever shuts his ears to the cry of the poor
>**Will also cry himself and *not* be heard!** (Proverbs 21:13)

Do Not Oppress the Poor

A poor man who oppresses (keeps down) the poor
    Is like a driving rain which leaves no food. (Proverbs 28:3)
Do not withhold good from those to whom it is due,
    When it is in the power of your hand to do so. (Proverbs 3:27)
Do not say to your neighbor,
   "Go, and come back,
   And tomorrow I will give it,"
    When you have it with you. (Proverbs 3:28)
Do not devise evil against your neighbor,
    For he dwells by you for *safety's* sake. (Proverbs 3:29)
Do not strive with a man without cause,
    If he has done you no harm. (Proverbs 3:30)
Do not envy the oppressor,
    And choose *none* of his ways; (Proverbs 3:31)
For the perverse person is an abomination to the LORD,
    But His secret counsel is with the upright. (Proverbs 3:32)
[The] treasures of wickedness profit nothing! (Proverbs 10:2)
He who oppresses the poor to increase his riches,
    And he who gives to the rich,
    Will *surely* come to poverty! (Proverbs 22:16)
He who oppresses the poor *reproaches* (finds fault with) his Maker,
    But he who honors Him has mercy on the needy. (Proverbs 14:31)
The poor man and the oppressor have this in common:
    The LORD gives light to the eyes of both. (Proverbs 29:13)
He who mocks the poor *reproaches* (finds fault with) his Maker;
    He who is glad at calamity (great misfortune)
    Will *not* go unpunished. (Proverbs 17:5)
The rich and the poor have this in common,
    The LORD is the maker of them all. (Proverbs 22:2)
There is a generation whose teeth are like swords,
    And whose fangs are like knives,
    To devour the poor from off the earth,
    And the needy from among men. (Proverbs 30:14)
The righteous considers the cause of the poor,
    But the wicked does not understand such knowledge. (Proverbs 29:7)
Do not remove the ancient landmark
    Which your fathers have set. (Proverbs 22:28)
Do not remove the ancient landmark,
    Nor enter the fields of the fatherless; (Proverbs 23:10)

For their Redeemer is mighty;
>   He will plead their cause against you. (Proverbs 23:11)

Do not rob the poor because he is poor,
>   Nor oppress (keep down) the afflicted (those who suffer)
>   At the gate; (Proverbs 22:22)

For the LORD will plead their cause,
>   And plunder the soul of those
>   who plunder them. (Proverbs 22:23)

Gain by Deceit

The plans of the diligent (hard-working) lead surely to plenty,
>   But [the plans] of everyone who is hasty,
>   Surely to poverty. (Proverbs 21:5)

Getting treasures by a lying tongue
>   Is the fleeting (swiftly passing) fantasy
>   Of those who seek death. (Proverbs 21:6)

Wealth gained by dishonesty will be diminished,
>   But he who gathers by labor will increase. (Proverbs 13:11)

One who increases his possessions
>   By usury (lending money at an excessive interest rate)
>   And extortion (taking money by force or threats)
>   Gathers it for him who will pity the poor. (Proverbs 28:8)

... The blameless will inherit good, (Proverbs 28:10)
[And] the wealth of the sinner
>   Is stored up for the righteous. (Proverbs 13:22)

Honest weights and scales are the LORD's;
>   All the weights in the bag are His work. (Proverbs 16:11)

Dishonest scales are an abomination to the LORD,
>   But a just weight is His delight. (Proverbs 11:1)

Diverse (purposefully inaccurate) weights and diverse measures,
>   They are both alike, an abomination to the LORD. (Proverbs 20:10)

Diverse weights are an abomination to the LORD,
>   And dishonest scales are not good. (Proverbs 20:23)

What is desired in a man is kindness,
>   **And a poor man is better than a liar!** (Proverbs 19:22)

Better is the poor who walks in his integrity
>   Than one perverse in his ways, though he be rich. (Proverbs 28:6)

...Ruthless men retain riches. (Proverbs 11:16)
"It is good for nothing", cries the buyer;
   But when he has gone his way, *then he boasts*! (Proverbs 20:14)
He who covers his sins *will not* prosper,
   But whoever confesses and forsakes them
   Will have mercy. (Proverbs 28:13)
A good name is to be chosen rather than great riches,
   Loving favor rather than silver and gold. (Proverbs 22:1)
The refining pot is for silver and the furnace for gold,
   And a man is valued by what *others* say of him. (Proverbs 27:21)

Fools and Their Money
There is desirable treasure,
   And oil in the dwelling of the wise,
   But a foolish man *squanders* it (spends it all)! (Proverbs 21:20)
In the house of the righteous there is much treasure,
   But in the revenue of the wicked is trouble. (Proverbs 15:6)
By knowledge the rooms are filled
   With all precious and pleasant riches. (Proverbs 24:4)
Through wisdom a house is built,
   And by understanding it is established; (Proverbs 24:3)
The wise woman builds her house,
   But the foolish [woman]
   Plucks it down with her hands (spends it)! (Proverbs 14:1)
Luxury is *not* fitting for a fool,
   Much less for a servant to rule over princes. (Proverbs 19:10)
Why is there in the hand of a fool the purchase price of wisdom,
   Since he has no heart for it? (Proverbs 17:16)
An inheritance gained hastily at the beginning
   Will not be blessed at the end. (Proverbs 20:21)
The wages of the wicked [are spent on] sin! (Proverbs 10:16)
He who loves pleasure will be a poor man;
   He who loves wine and oil *will not be rich*! (Proverbs 21:17)
Have you found honey?
   Eat only as much as you need,
   Lest you be filled with it and vomit. (Proverbs 25:16)

Do not mix with winebibbers,
    Or with gluttonous eaters of meat; (Proverbs 23:20)
For the drunkard and the glutton will come to poverty,
    And drowsiness will clothe a man with rags. (Proverbs 23:21)
...A companion of harlots *wastes* his wealth! (Proverbs 29:3)
Poverty and *shame* will come to him
    Who disdains correction (who thinks it beneath him),
    But he who regards a rebuke will be honored. (Proverbs 13:18)

The Bread of a Miser
Do not eat the bread of a miser,
    Nor desire his delicacies; (Proverbs 23:6)
For as he thinks in his heart, so is he.
    "Eat and drink!" he says to you,
    But his heart is not with you. (Proverbs 23:7)
The morsel you have eaten, you will vomit up,
    And waste your pleasant words. (Proverbs 23:8)

Treasures in Heaven
Lay not up for yourselves treasures upon earth,
    Where moth and rust doth corrupt,
    And where thieves break through and steal: (Matthew 6:19)
But lay up for yourselves treasures in heaven,
    Where neither moth nor rust doth corrupt,
    And where thieves do not break through nor steal: (Matthew 6:20)
For where your treasure is, *there will your heart be also*! (Matthew 6:21)

The Slothful Person

In the morning sow thy seed, and in the evening withhold not thy hand:
For thou knowest not whether shall prosper,
Either this or that,
Or whether they *both* shall be alike good! (Ecclesiastes 11:6)

The Field of the Slothful
I went by the field of the lazy man,
    And by the vineyard of the man
        Devoid of understanding; (Proverbs 24:30)
And there it was, all overgrown with thorns;
    Its surface was covered with nettles;
    Its stone wall was broken down. (Proverbs 24:31)
When I saw it, I considered it well;
    I looked on it and received instruction: (Proverbs 24:32)
A little sleep, a little slumber,
    A little folding of the hands to rest; (Proverbs 24:33)
So shall your poverty come on you like a prowler,
    And your need like an armed man. (Proverbs 24:34)

Consider the Ant
Go to the ant, you sluggard!
    Consider her ways and be wise, (Proverbs 6:6)
Which, having no captain,
    Overseer or ruler, (Proverbs 6:7)
Provides her supplies in the summer,
    And gathers her food in the harvest. (Proverbs 6:8)
How long will you slumber, O sluggard?
    When will you rise from your sleep? (Proverbs 6:9)
A little sleep, a little slumber,
    A little folding of the hands to sleep— (Proverbs 6:10)
So shall your poverty come on you like a prowler,
    And your need like an armed man. (Proverbs 6:11)

The Lazy Man
He who gathers in summer is a wise son;
    He who sleeps in harvest is a son who causes shame. (Proverbs 10:5)
The lazy man will not plow because of winter;
    He will beg during harvest and have nothing. (Proverbs 20:4)
The lazy man says, "There is a lion in the road!
    A fierce lion is in the streets!" (Proverbs 26:13)
The lazy man says, "There is a lion outside!
    I shall be slain in the streets!" (Proverbs 22:13)
Laziness casts one into a deep sleep,
    And an idle person *will* suffer hunger. (Proverbs 19:15)
As a door turns on its hinges,
    So does the lazy man on his bed. (Proverbs 26:14)
Do not love sleep, lest you come to poverty;
    Open your eyes, and you will be satisfied with bread. (Proverbs 20:13)
In all labor there is profit,
    But idle chatter leads only to poverty. (Proverbs 14:23)
The way of the lazy man is like a hedge of thorns,
    But the way of the upright is a highway. (Proverbs 15:19)
By much slothfulness the building decays;
    And through idleness of the hands
    The house drops through. (Ecclesiastes 10:18)
He who is slothful in his work
    Is a brother to him who is a great destroyer. (Proverbs 18:9)

The lazy man buries his hand in the bowl;
    It wearies him to bring it back to his mouth. (Proverbs 26:15)
A lazy man buries his hand in the bowl,
    And will not so much as bring it to his mouth again. (Proverbs 19:24)
The desire of the lazy man kills him,
    For his hands refuse to labor. (Proverbs 21:25)
He *covets greedily* all day long,
    But the righteous gives and does not spare. (Proverbs 21:26)
The soul of a lazy man desires, and has nothing;
    But the soul of the diligent shall be made rich. (Proverbs 13:4)
The hand of the diligent will rule,
    But the lazy man will be put to forced labor. (Proverbs 12:24)

The lazy man does not roast what he took in hunting,
>   **But the substance of a diligent man is *precious*!** (Proverbs 12:27)

He who tills his land will be satisfied with bread; (Proverbs 12:11)
He who tills his land will have plenty of bread,
>   But he who follows frivolity
>   Will have poverty enough! (Proverbs 28:19)

...If any [will] not work, neither should he eat. (II Thessalonians 3:10)

As vinegar to the teeth and smoke to the eyes,
>   So is the lazy man to those who send him. (Proverbs 10:26)

Do you see a man who excels in his work?
>   He will stand before kings;
>   He will not stand before unknown men. (Proverbs 22:29)

The lazy man is wiser in his own eyes
>   **Than seven men who can answer sensibly!** (Proverbs 26:16)

Debt and Surety

Owe no man *nothing*! (Romans 13:8)

A man devoid of (lacking) understanding shakes hands in a pledge,
    And becomes surety (assurance against loss, or collateral)
    For his friend. (Proverbs 17:18)
He who is surety for a stranger will suffer,
    But one who hates being surety is secure. (Proverbs 11:15)
Do not be one of those who shakes hands in a pledge,
    One of those who is surety for debts; (Proverbs 22:26)
If you have nothing with which to pay,
    Why should he take away your bed from under you? (Proverbs 22:27)

My son, if you become surety for your friend,
    If you have shaken hands in pledge for a stranger, (Proverbs 6:1)
You are *snared* by the words of your mouth;
    You are taken by the words of your mouth. (Proverbs 6:2)
So do this, my son, and deliver yourself;
    For you have come into the hand of your friend:
    Go and humble yourself;
    Plead with your friend. (Proverbs 6:3)
Give no sleep to your eyes,
    Nor slumber to your eyelids. (Proverbs 6:4)
Deliver yourself like a gazelle from the hand of the hunter,
    And like a bird from the hand
    Of the fowler (one who snares birds). (Proverbs 6:5)

Take the garment of one who is surety for a stranger,
    And hold it as a pledge when *it* is for a seductress. (Proverbs 20:16)
Take the garment of him who is surety for a stranger,
    And hold it in pledge when *he* is surety
    For a seductress. (Proverbs 27:13)

The wicked borrow and *do not* repay,
    But the righteous give generously! (Psalms 37:21)
Owe no man *nothing*! (Romans 13:8)
The rich rules over the poor,
    And the borrower is *servant* to the lender! (Proverbs 22:7)

Gifts and Bribes

...Every man is a friend to one who gives gifts. (Proverbs 19:6)

Many entreat (earnestly seek) the favor of the nobility,
    And *every man* is a friend to one who gives gifts. (Proverbs 19:6)
A man's gift makes room for him,
    And brings him before great men. (Proverbs 18:16)
A present is a precious stone in the eyes of its possessor;
    Wherever he turns, he prospers. (Proverbs 17:8)

A gift in secret pacifies anger,
    And a bribe behind the back, strong wrath. (Proverbs 21:14)
A wicked man accepts a bribe behind the back
    To pervert the ways of justice. (Proverbs 17:23)
The king establishes the land by justice,
    But he who receives bribes overthrows it. (Proverbs 29:4)
He who is greedy for gain troubles his own house,
    But he who hates bribes will live. (Proverbs 15:27)

Whoever falsely boasts of giving
    Is like clouds and wind without rain. (Proverbs 25:14)

Greed

A man with an evil eye hastens after riches,
    And does not consider that *poverty*
      Will come upon him. (Proverbs 28:22)

Proverbs 1
Shun Evil Council
10 My son, if sinners entice you,
    Do *not* consent.
11 If they say, "Come with us,
    Let us lie in wait to shed blood;
    Let us lurk secretly for the innocent without cause;
12 Let us swallow them alive like Sheol,
    And whole, like those who go down to the Pit;
13 We shall find all kinds of precious possessions,
    We shall fill our houses with spoil;
14 Cast in your lot among us,
    Let us all have one purse"—
15 My son, do *not* walk in the way with them,
    Keep your foot from their path;
16 For their feet run to evil,
    And they make haste to shed blood.
17 Surely, in vain the net is spread
    In the sight of any bird;
18 **But they lie in wait for *their own* blood,**
    They lurk secretly for *their own* lives!
19 **So are the ways of everyone who is greedy for gain;**
    It takes away the life of its owners.

Hastening to be Rich
A faithful man will abound with blessings,
   But he who hastens to be rich will not go unpunished. (Proverbs 28:20)
To show partiality is not good,
    Because for a piece of bread a man will transgress! (Proverbs 28:21)
A man with an *evil eye* hastens after riches,
    And does not consider that poverty
      Will come upon him. (Proverbs 28:22)

The wicked covet the catch of evil men, (Proverbs 12:12)
But the stomach of the wicked shall be in want. (Proverbs 13:25)
He who is greedy for gain troubles his own house,
    But he who hates bribes will live. (Proverbs 15:27)

The Thief

Whoever is a partner with a thief hates his own life. (Proverbs 29:24)

People, do not despise a thief
    If he steals to satisfy himself when he is starving. (Proverbs 6:30)
Yet when he is found, he must restore sevenfold;
    He may have to give up all the substance of his house. (Proverbs 6:31)

Do not lie in wait, O wicked man, against the dwelling of the righteous;
    Do not plunder his resting place; (Proverbs 24:15)
For a righteous man may fall seven times
    And rise again,
    But the wicked shall fall by calamity. (Proverbs 24:16)
Whoever robs his father or his mother,
    And says, "It is no transgression,"
    The same is companion to a destroyer. (Proverbs 28:24)

Dishonest scales are an abomination to the LORD,
    But a just weight is His delight. (Proverbs 11:1)
Bread gained by deceit is sweet to a man,
    But afterward his mouth will be filled with gravel. (Proverbs 20:17)
Getting treasures by a lying tongue
    Is the fleeting fantasy of those who seek death; (Proverbs 21:6)
…And a poor man is better than a liar! (Proverbs 19:22)

Whoever is a partner with a thief hates his own life;
    He swears to tell the truth, but reveals nothing. (Proverbs 29:24)

Friendship

Go from the presence of a foolish man,
    When you do not perceive in him
    The lips of knowledge! (Proverbs 14:7)

Choosing Friends Wisely
The righteous should choose his friends *carefully*,
    For the way of the wicked leads them astray! (Proverbs 12:26)
Folly is *joyous* to him who is destitute of (lacks) **wisdom,** (KJV)
    But a man of understanding walks uprightly. (Proverbs 15:21)
He who walks with wise men will be wise,
    But the companion of fools will be *destroyed*! (Proverbs 13:20)
…It is an abomination to fools to depart from evil. (Proverbs 13:19)
Go from the presence of a foolish man,
    When you do not perceive in him
    The lips of knowledge! (Proverbs 14:7)

Being a Friend
A friend loves at all times,
    And a brother is born for adversity. (Proverbs 17:17)
As iron sharpens iron,
    So a man sharpens the countenance (facial expression)
    Of his friend. (Proverbs 27:17)
A man who has friends must himself be friendly,
    And there is a friend
    Who sticks closer than a brother. (Proverbs 18:24)
Do not forsake your own friend or your father's friend,
    Nor go to your brother's house
    In the day of your calamity (great misfortune);
    Better is a neighbor nearby than a brother far away. (Proverbs 27:10)

The Poor Man's Friends
All the brothers of the poor hate him;
    How much more do his friends go far from him!
    He may pursue them with words,
    Yet they abandon him! (Proverbs 19:7)

Enemies and Strife

Do *not* rejoice when your enemy falls,
    And do *not* let your heart be glad when he stumbles. (Proverbs 24:17)

Strife with Neighbors
The soul of the wicked desires evil;
    His neighbor finds no favor in his eyes. (Proverbs 21:10)
Do not devise evil against your neighbor,
    For he dwells by you for *safety's* sake. (Proverbs 3:29)
Do not strive with a man without cause,
    If he has done you no harm. (Proverbs 3:30)
He who is devoid of (lacking) wisdom *despises* (loathes) his neighbor:
    But a man of understanding
    Holds his peace [with his neighbor]. (Proverbs 11:12)
Seldom set foot in your neighbor's house,
    Lest he become weary of you and hate you. (Proverbs 25:17)
Hatred stirs up strife (quarrels),
    But love covers all sins. (Proverbs 10:12)
The beginning of strife (quarrels) is like releasing water;
    Therefore stop contention (disputes)
    Before a quarrel starts. (Proverbs 17:14)
It is honorable for a man to stop striving (quarreling),
    Since *any fool* can start a quarrel! (Proverbs 20:3)
He who loves transgression (sin) loves strife (quarrels),
    And he who exalts his gate seeks destruction. (Proverbs 17:19)
For as the churning of milk produces butter,
    And wringing the nose produces blood,
    So the forcing of wrath produces strife. (Proverbs 30:33)
Casting lots causes contentions (disputes) to cease,
    And keeps the mighty apart. (Proverbs 18:18)
A brother offended is harder to win than a strong city,
    And contentions (disputes)
    Are like the bars of a castle. (Proverbs 18:19)

Enemies
Do *not* say, "I will recompense evil";
> Wait for the LORD, and *He* will save you. (Proverbs 20:22)

Do *not* rejoice when your enemy falls!...
> **And do *not* let your heart be glad when he stumbles;** (Proverbs 24:17)

Lest the LORD see it, and it displease Him,
> And He turn away His wrath from him. (Proverbs 24:18)

... He who is *glad* at calamity (great misfortune)
> Will not go unpunished. (Proverbs 17:5)

If your enemy is hungry, give him bread to eat;
> And if he is thirsty, give him water to drink; (Proverbs 25:21)

For so you will heap coals of fire on his head,
> And the LORD will reward you. (Proverbs 25:22)

When a man's ways please the LORD,
> **He makes *even his enemies* to be at peace with him!** (Proverbs 16:7)

Quarrels Not Your Own
He who passes by and meddles in a quarrel not his own
> **Is like one who takes a dog by the ears!** (Proverbs 26:17)

The Words of a Person's Mouth

**If any man offend not in word, the same is a perfect man,
And able also to bridle the whole body.** (James 3:2)

The Fruit of a Person's Words
Death and life are in the power of the tongue,
    And those who love it will eat its fruit. (Proverbs 18:21)
A man's stomach shall be satisfied from the fruit of his mouth;
    From the produce of his lips he shall be filled. (Proverbs 18:20)
A man has joy by the answer of his mouth,
    And a word spoken in due season, how good it is! (Proverbs 15:23)
He who gives a right answer kisses the lips. (Proverbs 24:26)
Pleasant words are like a honeycomb,
    Sweetness to the soul and health to the bones. (Proverbs 16:24)
By long forbearance a ruler is persuaded,
    And a gentle tongue breaks a bone. (Proverbs 25:15)
A word fitly spoken is like apples of gold
    In settings of silver. (Proverbs 25:11)
Whoever guards his mouth and tongue
    Keeps his soul from troubles! (Proverbs 21:23)
Whoever keeps the fig tree will eat its fruit;
    So he who waits on his master will be honored. (Proverbs 27:18)
A man shall eat well by the fruit of his mouth,
    But the soul of the unfaithful feeds on violence. (Proverbs 13:2**)**
A wholesome tongue is a tree of life,
    But perverseness in [the tongue] breaks the spirit. (Proverbs 15:4)
He who guards his mouth preserves his life,
    But he who opens wide his lips shall have destruction. (Proverbs 13:3)

The Mouth of the Wise and Foolish
The words of a man's mouth are deep waters;
    The wellspring of wisdom is a flowing brook. (Proverbs 18:4)
The tongue of the wise promotes health (Proverbs 12:18)
[And]…a faithful ambassador brings health. (Proverbs 13:17)
There is gold and a multitude of rubies,
    But the lips of knowledge are a *precious* jewel! (Proverbs 20:15)

He who has knowledge spares his words,
    And a man of understanding is of a *calm* spirit! (Proverbs 17:27)
Even a fool is counted wise when he holds his peace;
    When he shuts his lips, he is considered perceptive. (Proverbs 17:28)
A soft answer turns away wrath,
    But a harsh word *stirs up anger*! (Proverbs 15:1)
The lips of the wise disperse (spread) knowledge,
    But the heart of the fool does not do so. (Proverbs 15:7)
The tongue of the wise uses knowledge rightly,
    But the mouth of fools pours forth *foolishness*. (Proverbs 15:2)
The words of a wise man's mouth are *gracious*;
    But the lips of a fool will swallow up himself. (Ecclesiastes 10:12)
If a wise man contends with a foolish man,
    Whether the fool *rages* or *laughs*, there is *no* peace. (Proverbs 29:9)
The words of wise men are heard in quiet
    More than the cry of him that rules among fools. (Ecclesiastes 9:17)
The mouth of the foolish is near destruction; (Proverbs 10:14)
A fool's mouth *is his destruction*,
    And his lips are the snare of his soul. (Proverbs 18:7)
Like the legs of the lame that hang limp
    Is a proverb in the mouth of fools. (Proverbs 26:7)
Like a thorn that goes into the hand of a drunkard
    Is a proverb in the mouth of fools. (Proverbs 26:9)
He who sends a message by the hand of a fool
    Cuts off his own feet and drinks violence. (Proverbs 26:6)

The Mouth of the Righteous
What is desired in a man is kindness; (Proverbs 19:22)
The mouth of the righteous is a well of life, (Proverbs 10:11)
[And it] brings forth wisdom. (Proverbs 10:31)
The tongue of the righteous is choice silver. (Proverbs 10:20)
...The tongue of the wise promotes health, (Proverbs 12:18)
[And] counselors of peace have joy. (Proverbs 12:20)
The lips of the righteous know what is acceptable, (Proverbs 10:32)
[And] a righteous man *hates* lying! (Proverbs 13:5)
Lying lips are an *abomination* to the LORD,
    But those who deal truthfully are His delight. (Proverbs 12:22)
...The mouth of the upright will deliver them, (Proverbs 12:6)
[And] the truthful lip shall be established forever. (Proverbs 12:19)

The heart of the righteous *studies* how to answer... (Proverbs 15:28)
[And] the lips of the wise will preserve them. (Proverbs 14:3)
The preparations of the heart belong to man,
    But the answer of the tongue is from the LORD. (Proverbs 16:1)
A man will be satisfied
    With good by the fruit of his mouth. (Proverbs 12:14)
The fruit of the righteous is a tree of life,
    And he who wins souls is wise. (Proverbs 11:30)

The Mouth of the Wicked
A worthless person, a wicked man,
    Walks with a perverse mouth; (Proverbs 6:12)
...The mouth of the wicked [knows] what is perverse, (Proverbs 10:32)
And he who has a perverse tongue *falls into evil*! (Proverbs 17:20)
Better is the poor who walks in his integrity
    Than one who is perverse in his lips, and is a fool. (Proverbs 19:1)
...A prating fool (one who gives away secrets) will fall, (Proverbs 10:10)
[And] the perverse tongue will be cut out. (Proverbs 10:31)
... The mouth of the wicked pours forth evil; (Proverbs 15:28)
He moves his lips and brings about evil. (Proverbs 16:30) (KJV)
He devises evil continually,
    He sows discord (disagreements). (Proverbs 6:14)
[His] lips talk of troublemaking. (Proverbs 24:2)
An ungodly man digs up evil,
    And it is on his lips like a burning fire. (Proverbs 16:27)
An evildoer gives heed to false lips;
    A liar listens eagerly to a spiteful (begrudging) tongue, (Proverbs 17:4)
[And] the simple (fool) believes every word. (Proverbs 14:15)
A perverse man sows strife (quarrels),
    And a whisperer (one who spreads gossip)
    Separates the best of friends! (Proverbs 16:28)
... The counsels of the wicked are deceitful; (Proverbs 12:5)
...The kisses of an enemy are deceitful, (Proverbs 27:6)
[And] a false witness [declares] deceit. (Proverbs 12:17)
There is one who speaks like the piercings of a sword, (Proverbs 12:18)
[And] the tender mercies of the wicked are cruel. (Proverbs 12:10)
The words of the wicked are, "Lie in wait for blood." (Proverbs 12:6)

The wicked is ensnared
   By the transgression (sin) of his lips, (Proverbs 12:13)
[And] a wicked messenger falls into trouble. (Proverbs 13:17)
...Violence covers the mouth
   Of the wicked (Proverbs 10:6) (Proverbs 10:11)
For [his] heart devises violence. (Proverbs 24:2)
There is a generation that curses its father,
   And does not bless its mother. (Proverbs 30:11)
The eye that mocks his father,
   And scorns (loathes) obedience to his mother,
   The ravens of the valley will pick it out,
   And the young eagles will eat it. (Proverbs 30:17)
Whoever curses his father or his mother,
   His lamp will be put out in deep darkness. (Proverbs 20:20)

Truth
He who speaks truth declares righteousness. (Proverbs 12:17)
Like the cold of snow in time of harvest
   Is a faithful messenger to those who send him,
   For he refreshes the soul of his masters. (Proverbs 25:13)
Confidence in an unfaithful man in time of trouble
   Is like a bad tooth and a foot out of joint. (Proverbs 25:19)

Lies and Deceit
He who speaks truth declares righteousness, (Proverbs 12:17)
But a lying tongue is but for a moment. (Proverbs 12:19)
A lying tongue *hates* those who are crushed by it,
   And a flattering mouth works ruin. (Proverbs 26:28)
A man who flatters his neighbor
   Spreads a net for his feet! (Proverbs 29:5)
The hypocrite with his mouth destroys his neighbor; (Proverbs 11:9)
He who blesses his friend with a loud voice, rising early in the morning,
   It will be counted a curse to him. (Proverbs 27:14)
Put away from you a deceitful (lying) mouth,
   And put perverse lips far from you. (Proverbs 2:24)

He who hates, *disguises it* with his lips,
    And lays up deceit within himself. (Proverbs 26:24)
When he speaks kindly, do not believe him,
    For there are seven abominations in his heart; (Proverbs 26:25)
Though his hatred is covered by deceit,
    His wickedness will be revealed before the assembly. (Proverbs 26:26)
Whoever digs a pit will fall into it,
    And he who rolls a stone will have it roll back on him. (Proverbs 26:27)
Fervent lips (showing great warmth) with a wicked heart
    Are like earthenware (clay pots) covered with
    Silver dross (the slag from molten metal). (Proverbs 26:23)

The False Witness
A faithful witness does not lie,
    But a false witness will utter lies. (Proverbs 14:5)
A true witness delivers souls,
    But a deceitful witness speaks lies. (Proverbs 14:25)
... A false witness [declares] deceit; (Proverbs 12: 17)
A man who bears false witness against his neighbor
    Is like a club, a sword, and a sharp arrow. (Proverbs 25:18)
A false witness will not go unpunished,
    And he who speaks lies will not escape. (Proverbs 19:5)
A false witness will not go unpunished,
    And he who speaks lies shall perish. (Proverbs 19:9)
A false witness shall perish,
    But the man who hears him will speak endlessly. (Proverbs 21:28)
A disreputable witness scorns (loathes) justice,
    And the mouth of the wicked
    Devours (feeds ravenously on) iniquity. (Proverbs 19:28)
Do not be a witness against your neighbor without cause,
    For would you deceive with your lips? (Proverbs 24:28)
Do not say, "I will do to him just as he has done to me;
    I will render to the man according to his work." (Proverbs 24:29)

Gossip

A talebearer (one who spreads gossip) reveals secrets,
    But he who is of a faithful spirit conceals a matter. (Proverbs 11:13)
He who covers a transgression seeks love,
    But he who repeats a matter *separates friends*! (Proverbs 17:9)
Whoever hides hatred has lying lips,
    And whoever spreads slander (lies that hurt another's reputation)
    Is a fool. (Proverbs 10:18)
The north wind brings forth rain,
    And a backbiting (slandering) tongue
    An angry countenance (expression). (Proverbs 25:23)
Where there is no wood, the fire goes out;
    And where there is no talebearer (gossip),
    Strife (quarrels) ceases. (Proverbs 26:20)
As charcoal is to burning coals, and wood to fire,
    So is a contentious (disputing) man
    To kindle strife (quarrels). (Proverbs 26:21)
The words of a talebearer (gossip)
    Are like tasty trifles (unimportant matters),
    And they go down
    Into the inmost body. (Proverbs 18:8) (Proverbs 26:22)
He who goes about as a talebearer (gossip) reveals secrets;
    Therefore do not associate with one
    Who flatters with his lips. (Proverbs 20:19)
A prating fool (one who reveals secrets) *will fall*. (Proverbs 10:8)

Do not go hastily to court;
    For what will you do in the end,
    When your neighbor has put you to shame? (Proverbs 25:8)
Debate your case with your neighbor,
    And do *not* disclose the secret to another; (Proverbs 25:9)
Lest he who hears it expose your shame,
    And your reputation be ruined. (Proverbs 25:10)

Speaking Evil of Others
Do not malign (speak evil of) a servant to his master,
> Lest he curse you, and you be found guilty. (Proverbs 30:10)

Curse not the king, no not in thy thought;
> And curse not the rich in thy bedchamber:
> For a bird of the air shall carry the voice,
> And that which hath wings shall tell the matter. (Ecclesiastes 10:20)

Self-Praise
It is not good to eat much honey;
> **So to seek one's own glory *is not glory*!** (Proverbs 25:27)

Let *another man* praise you, and not your own mouth;
> **A stranger, *and not your own lips*!** (Proverbs 27:2)

Better is the one who is slighted but has a servant,
> Than he who honors himself but lacks bread. (Proverbs 12:9)

If you have been foolish in exalting yourself,
> **Or if you have devised evil,**
> **Put your hand on your mouth!** (Proverbs 30:32)

Anger
He who has knowledge spares his words,
> And a man of understanding is of a *calm* spirit. (Proverbs 17:27)

The discretion of a man makes him *slow to anger*,
> And his glory is to overlook a transgression. (Proverbs 19:11)

He who is slow to anger is better than the mighty,
> And he who rules his spirit
> [Is better] than he who takes a city. (Proverbs 16:32)

Whoever has no rule over his own spirit
> Is like a city broken down, without walls. (Proverbs 25:28)

A wise man fears [the LORD] and departs from evil,
> But a fool rages and is self-confident. (Proverbs 14:16)

A wrathful man stirs up strife (quarrels),
> But he who is slow to anger
> Allays (alleviates) contention. (Proverbs 15:18)

Scoffers (mockers) set a city aflame,
    But wise men turn away wrath. (Proverbs 29:8)
A fool's wrath is known *at once*,
    But a prudent man (one with sound judgment)
    Covers shame. (Proverbs 12: 16)

A quick-tempered man acts *foolishly*! (Proverbs 14:17)
He who is slow to wrath has great understanding,
    But he who is impulsive *exalts* folly. (Proverbs 14:29)
An angry man stirs up strife (quarrels),
    And a furious man abounds in transgression. (Proverbs 29:22)
In the multitude of words *sin is not lacking*,
    But he who restrains his lips is wise. (Proverbs 10:19)
Even a fool is counted wise when he holds his peace;
    When he shuts his lips, he is considered perceptive. (Proverbs 17:28)
A stone is heavy and sand is weighty,
    But a fool's wrath is heavier than both of them. (Proverbs 27:3)
Wrath is cruel and anger a torrent (a swift, violent stream),
    But who is able to stand before jealousy? (Proverbs 27: 4)
A man of great wrath will suffer punishment;
    For if you rescue him, you will have to do it *again*! (Proverbs 19:19)

Make no friendship with an angry man,
    And with a furious man do not go, (Proverbs 22:24)
Lest you learn his ways
    And set a snare for your soul! (Proverbs 22:25)

Discernment
The first one to plead his cause seems right,
    Until his neighbor comes and examines him. (Proverbs 18:17)
He who answers a matter...before he hears it,
    It is *folly* and *shame* to him! (Proverbs 18:13)

Vows
Walk prudently (be of sound judgment) when you go to the house of God;
    And draw near to *hear* rather than to give the sacrifice of fools,
        For they do not know that they do evil! (Ecclesiastes 5:1)
Do not be rash with your mouth,
    And let not your heart utter *anything* hastily before God!
    For God is in heaven, and you on earth;
    Therefore let your words be few! (Ecclesiastes 5:2)
For a dream comes through much activity,
    And a fool's voice is known by his *many* words. (Ecclesiastes 5:3)
When you make a vow to God, do *not* delay to pay it;
    For He has no pleasure in fools.
        Pay what you have vowed— (Ecclesiastes 5:4)
Better not to vow...than to vow and not pay! (Ecclesiastes 5:5)
Do not let your mouth cause your flesh to sin,
    Nor say before the messenger of God that it was an error.
    Why should God be angry at your excuse
    And *destroy* the work of your hands? (Ecclesiastes 5:6)
For in the multitude of dreams and many words there is also vanity.
    But fear God. (Ecclesiastes 5:7)
It is a snare for a man to devote rashly something as holy,
    And afterward to reconsider his vows. (Proverbs 20:25)

The Heart

**A merry heart does good, like medicine,
    But a broken spirit dries the bones.** (Proverbs 17:22)

Gladness and Sadness of the Heart
Anxiety in the heart of man causes *depression*,
    But a good word makes it glad. (Proverbs 12:25)
Hope deferred makes the heart *sick*,
    But when the desire comes, it is a tree of life. (Proverbs 13:12)
A desire accomplished is *sweet* to the soul. (Proverbs 13:19)
The fear of man brings a snare,
    But whoever trusts in the LORD shall be safe. (Proverbs 29:25)
The eyes of the LORD preserve knowledge,
    But He overthrows the words of the faithless. (Proverbs 22:12)
He who heeds the word wisely will find good,
    And whoever trusts in the LORD, *happy* is he! (Proverbs 16:20)

All the days of the afflicted (those who suffer) are evil,
    But he who is of a merry heart has a continual feast. (Proverbs 15:15)
Ointment and perfume delight the heart,
    And the sweetness of a man's friend gives delight
    By hearty counsel. (Proverbs 27:9)
As cold water to a weary soul,
    So is good news from a far country. (Proverbs 25:25)
The light of the eyes *rejoices* the heart,
    And a good report makes the bones healthy. (Proverbs 15:30)

A merry heart makes a cheerful countenance (facial expression),
    But by sorrow of the heart...the spirit is broken. (Proverbs 15:13)
The spirit of a man will sustain him in sickness,
    But who can bear a broken spirit? (Proverbs 18:14)
A merry heart does good, like medicine,
    But a broken spirit dries the bones. (Proverbs 17:22)
A sound heart is life to the body,
    But *envy* is rottenness to the bones. (Proverbs 14:30)
Happy is the man who is always reverent (respectful),
    But he who hardens his heart will fall into calamity. (Proverbs 28:14)

The heart knows its own bitterness,
>   And a stranger *does not* share its joy. (Proverbs 14:10)
> ***Even in laughter* the heart may sorrow,**
>   And the end of mirth may be grief. (Proverbs 14:13)
> The heart of the wise is in the house of mourning;
>   But the heart of fools is in the house of mirth. (Ecclesiastes 7:4)

> Like one who takes away a garment in cold weather,
>   And like vinegar on soda,
>   Is one who sings songs to a heavy heart. (Proverbs 25:20)

Plans of the Heart

> A man's heart plans his way,
>   But the LORD directs his steps. (Proverbs 16:9)
> The preparations of the heart belong to man,
>   But the answer of the tongue is from the LORD. (Proverbs 16:1)
> There are many plans in a man's heart,
>   Nevertheless the LORD's counsel—that will stand. (Proverbs 19:21)
> The lot is cast into the lap,
>   But its every decision is from the LORD. (Proverbs 16:33)

God Searches the Heart

> The spirit of a man *is* the lamp of the LORD,
>   Searching all the inner depths of his heart. (Proverbs 20:27)
> **Every way of a man is right *in his own eyes*,**
>   But the LORD weighs the hearts. (Proverbs 21:2)
> The refining pot is for silver and the furnace for gold,
>   But the LORD tests the hearts. (Proverbs 17:3)
> **As in water… face reflects face,**
>   **So a man's heart reveals the man!** (Proverbs 27:19)
> Hell and Destruction are before the LORD;
>   So how much more the hearts of the sons of men! (Proverbs 15:11)
> **Keep your heart with all diligence;**
>   **For out of it are the issues of life!** (Proverbs 4:23)

The Wise and Foolish Hearts
A wise man's heart is at his right hand;
    But a fool's heart at his left. (Ecclesiastes 10:2)
The heart of the wise teaches his mouth,
    And adds learning to his lips. (Proverbs 16:23)
Whoso keeps the commandment shall feel no evil thing:
    And a wise man's heart discerns *both*
    Time and judgment! (Ecclesiastes 8:5)
The heart of him who has understanding seeks knowledge,
    But the mouth of fools feeds on foolishness. (Proverbs 15:14)
A fool has no delight in understanding,
    But in expressing *his own* heart! (Proverbs 18:2)
A fool vents *all* his feelings,
    But a wise man holds them back. (Proverbs 29:11)
...A fool lays open his folly, (Proverbs 13:16)
[And] what is in the heart of fools is made known. (Proverbs 14:33)
... The heart of fools proclaims foolishness. (Proverbs 12:23)
He who trusts in his own heart *is a fool*,
    But whoever walks wisely will be delivered. (Proverbs 28:26)
The foolishness of a man twists his way,
    And his heart *frets* against (is angry with) the LORD. (Proverbs 19:3)
Hear, my son, and be wise;
    And guide your heart in the way. (Proverbs 23:19)
Counsel in the heart of man is like deep water,
    But a man of understanding will draw it out. (Proverbs 20:5)

The Heart of the Wicked
The heart of the wicked is worth little, (Proverbs 10:20)
[And] he who perverts his ways will become known. (Proverbs 10:9)
Perversity is in his heart, (Proverbs 6:14)
[And]...the wicked shall be filled with evil. (Proverbs 12:21)
...He who is of a perverse heart will be despised; (Proverbs 12:8)
Those who are of a perverse heart
    Are an abomination to the LORD. (Proverbs 11:20)

***Deceit* is in the heart of those who devise evil,** (Proverbs 12:20)
[And] the wicked man does deceptive work. (Proverbs 11:18)
He who has a deceitful heart finds no good,
    And he who has a perverse tongue falls into evil. (Proverbs 17:20)

He who plots to do evil
    Will be called a schemer. (Proverbs 24:8)
The soul of the wicked desires evil;
    His neighbor finds *no* favor in his eyes. (Proverbs 21:10)
He who is of a proud heart stirs up strife (quarrels),
    But he who trusts in the LORD will be prospered. (Proverbs 28:25)
…Violence covers
    The mouth of the wicked (Proverbs 10:6) (Proverbs 10:11)
For [his] heart devises violence. (Proverbs 24:2)

Where there is no revelation,
    The people cast off restraint; (Proverbs 29:18)
Those who forsake the law *praise* the wicked! (Proverbs 28:4)
The backslider in heart will be filled with *his own* ways,
    But a good man will be satisfied from above. (Proverbs 14:14)
[The LORD] casts away the desire of the wicked. (Proverbs 10:3)
Do not let your heart *envy* sinners,
    But be zealous (enthusiastic)
    For the fear of the LORD all the day; (Proverbs 23:17)
For surely there is a hereafter,
    And your hope will not be cut off. (Proverbs 23:18)

Adultery and Fornication

For *this* is the will of God...
  That you should abstain from fornication: (I Thessalonians 4:3)
Let not fornication...be named *once* among you... (Ephesians 5:3)
...For it is a *shame* even to speak of those things
  Which are done of them in secret. (Ephesians 5:12)

Proverbs 5
The Peril of Adultery
[1] My son, pay attention to my wisdom;
  Lend your ear to my understanding,
[2] That you may preserve discretion,
  And your lips may keep knowledge.
[3] For the lips of an immoral woman drip honey,
  And her mouth is smoother than oil;
[4] But in the end she is bitter as wormwood,
  Sharp as a two-edged sword.
[5] Her feet go down to death,
  Her steps lay hold of hell.
[6] Lest you ponder her path of life—
  Her ways are unstable;
  You do not know them.
[7] Therefore hear me now, my children,
  And do not depart from the words of my mouth.
[8] Remove your way *far* from her,
  And do not go near the door of her house,
[9] Lest you give your honor to others,
  And your years to the cruel one;
[10] Lest aliens be filled with your wealth,
  And your labors go to the house of a foreigner;
[11] And you mourn at last,
  When your flesh and your body are consumed,
[12] And say:
  "How I have hated instruction,
  And my heart despised correction!
[13] I have not obeyed the voice of my teachers,
  Nor inclined my ear to those who instructed me!

¹⁴ I was on the verge of total ruin,
    In the midst of the assembly and congregation."
¹⁵ Drink water from your own cistern,
    And running water from your own well.
¹⁶ Should your fountains be dispersed abroad,
    Streams of water in the streets?
¹⁷ Let them be only your own,
    And *not* for strangers with you.
¹⁸ Let your fountain be blessed,
    And rejoice with the wife of your youth.
¹⁹ As a loving deer and a graceful doe,
    Let her breasts satisfy you at all times;
    And always be enraptured (delighted) with her love.
²⁰ For why should you, my son, be enraptured by an immoral woman,
    And be embraced in the arms of a seductress?
²¹ For the ways of man are before the eyes of the LORD,
    And He ponders all his paths.
²² His own iniquities entrap the wicked man,
    And he is caught in the cords of his sin.
²³ He shall die for lack of instruction,
    And in the greatness of his folly *he shall go astray*.

Proverbs 6
Beware of Adultery

²⁴ [Your father's commandment will] keep you from the evil woman,
    From the flattering tongue of a seductress.
²⁵ **Do not lust after her *beauty* in your heart,**
    Nor let her allure you with her eyelids.

As a ring of gold in a swine's snout,
    So is a lovely woman who lacks discretion. (Proverbs 11:22)

²⁶ For by means of a harlot
    A man is reduced to a crust of bread;
    And an adulteress will *prey* upon his precious life! (KJV)

[And]...the leech has two daughters— Give and Give! (Proverbs 30:15)

Whoever loves wisdom makes his father rejoice,
    But a companion of harlots *wastes* his wealth! (Proverbs 29:3)

²⁷ Can a man take fire to his bosom,
  And his clothes not be burned?
²⁸ Can one walk on hot coals,
  And his feet not be seared?
²⁹ So is he who goes in to his neighbor's wife;
  Whoever touches her *shall not* be innocent!
³² **Whoever commits adultery with a woman lacks understanding;**
  He who does so *destroys* his own soul!
³³ Wounds and dishonor he will get,
  And his reproach (shame) will *not* be wiped away.
³⁴ For jealousy is a husband's fury;
  Therefore he will not spare in the day of vengeance.
³⁵ He will accept no recompense,
  Nor will he be appeased though you give many gifts.

Proverbs 7
The Crafty Harlot

¹ My son, keep my words,
  And treasure my commands within you.
² Keep my commands and live,
  And my law as the apple of your eye.
³ Bind them on your fingers;
  Write them on the tablet of your heart.
⁴ Say to wisdom, "You are my sister,"
  And call understanding your nearest kin,
⁵ That they may keep you from the immoral woman,
  From the seductress who flatters with her words.
⁶ For at the window of my house
  I looked through my lattice,
⁷ And saw among the simple,
  I perceived among the youths,
  A young man devoid of (lacking) understanding,
⁸ Passing along the street near her corner;
  And he took the path to her house
⁹ In the twilight, in the evening,
  In the black and dark night.
¹⁰ And there a woman met him,
  With the attire (clothing) of a harlot, and a crafty heart.

¹¹ She was loud and rebellious,
　　Her feet would not stay at home.
¹² At times she was outside, at times in the open square,
　　Lurking at every corner.
¹³ So she caught him and kissed him;
　　With an impudent (shamelessly bold) face she said to him:
¹⁴ "I have peace offerings with me;
　　Today I have paid my vows.
¹⁵ So I came out to meet you,
　　Diligently to seek your face,
　　And I have found you.
¹⁶ I have spread my bed with tapestry,
　　Colored coverings of Egyptian linen.
¹⁷ I have perfumed my bed
　　With myrrh, aloes, and cinnamon.
¹⁸ Come, let us take our fill of love until morning;
　　Let us delight ourselves with love.
¹⁹ For my husband is not at home;
　　He has gone on a long journey;
²⁰ He has taken a bag of money with him,
　　And will come home on the appointed day."
²¹ With her enticing speech she caused him to yield,
　　With her flattering lips she seduced him.
²² Immediately he went after her, as an ox goes to the slaughter,
　　Or as a fool to the correction of the stocks,
²³ Till an arrow struck his liver.
　　As a bird hastens to the snare,
　　He did not know it would cost his life.
²⁴ Now therefore, listen to me, my children;
　　Pay attention to the words of my mouth:
²⁵ Do not let your heart turn aside to her ways,
　　Do not stray into her paths;
²⁶ For she has cast down many wounded,
　　And all who were slain by her were strong men.
²⁷ **Her house is the way to *hell*,**
　　Descending to the chambers of death.

Do not give your strength to women,
　　Nor your ways to that which *destroys* kings! (Proverbs 31:3)

Proverbs 9
The Foolish Woman
[13] A *foolish* woman is clamorous (loud, demanding and complaining);
  She is simple, and knows nothing.
[14] For she sits at the door of her house,
  On a seat by the highest places of the city,
[15] To call to those who pass by,
  Who go straight on their way:
[16] "Whoever is simple, let him turn in here";
  And as for him who lacks understanding, she says to him,
[17] "Stolen water is sweet,
  And bread eaten in secret is pleasant."
[18] But he does not know that the dead are there,
  That her guests *are in the depths of hell.*

The mouth of an immoral woman is a deep pit;
  He who is abhorred (hated) by the LORD
  Will fall there. (Proverbs 22:14)
For a harlot is a deep pit,
  And a seductress is a narrow well. (Proverbs 23:27)
She also lies in wait as for a victim,
  And increases the unfaithful among men. (Proverbs 23:28)

I find more bitter than death the woman,
  Whose heart is snares and nets, and her hands as bands:
  Whoso pleases God shall escape from her;
  But the sinner shall be taken by her. (Ecclesiastes 7:26)

This is the way of an adulterous woman:
  She eats and wipes her mouth,
  And says, "I have done no wickedness." (Proverbs 30:20)

Adultery of the Heart
Ye have heard that it was said by them of old time,
    Thou shalt not commit adultery: (Matthew 5:27)
But I say unto you, that whosoever looks on a woman to lust after her
    Has committed adultery with her already in his heart. (Matthew 5:28)

I made a covenant with my eyes not to look with lust
    At a young woman. (Job 31:1) (NLT)

Hell and Destruction are never full;
    So the eyes of man are *never* satisfied! (Proverbs 27:20)

Flee fornication. Every sin that a man doeth is without the body;
    But he that commits fornication
    Sins against his own body. (I Corinthians 6:18)

You adulterers and adulteresses,
    Know you not that the friendship of the world is enmity with God?
    Whosoever therefore will be a friend of the world
    Is the *enemy* of God! (James 4:4)

Be not deceived [by the foolish actions of others]: * See: Fools Delight in Sin - pg. 30
    Neither fornicators... nor adulterers... (I Corinthians 6:9)
...Shall inherit the kingdom of God! (I Corinthians 6:10)

Women

Charm is *deceitful* and beauty is *passing*,
    But a woman who fears the LORD,
      She shall be *praised*! (Proverbs 31:30)

Finding a Wife
He who finds a wife finds a good thing,
    And obtains favor from the LORD. (Proverbs 18:22)
Houses and riches are an inheritance from fathers,
    But a prudent wife (one who uses sound judgment)
    Is from the LORD. (Proverbs 19:14)
A gracious woman retains honor. (Proverbs 11:16)

The Foolish Wife
The wise woman builds her house,
    But the foolish [woman]
      Plucks it down with her hands (spends it)! (Proverbs 14:1)
A foolish woman
    Is clamorous (loud, demanding and complaining). (Proverbs 9:13)
An excellent wife is the crown of her husband,
    But she who causes shame
    Is like *rottenness* in his bones! (Proverbs 12:4)
As a ring of gold in a swine's snout,
    So is a lovely woman
      Who lacks discretion (sound judgment). (Proverbs 11:22)

The Contentious Wife
… The contentions (disputes) of a wife
    Are a continual dripping. (Proverbs 19:13)
A continual dripping on a very rainy day
    And a contentious (disputing) woman are alike; (Proverbs 27:15)
Whoever restrains her restrains the wind,
    And grasps oil with his right hand. (Proverbs 27:16)
Better to dwell in a corner of a housetop,
    Than in a house shared
     With a contentious woman. (Proverbs 21:9) (Proverbs 25:24)
Better to dwell in the wilderness,
    Than with a contentious and angry woman. (Proverbs 21:19)

Proverbs 31
The Virtuous Wife
[10] Who can find a virtuous (moral) wife?
> **For her worth is *far above* rubies!**

[11] The heart of her husband safely trusts her;
> **So he will have *no lack* of gain!**

[12] She does him good and not evil
> All the days of her life.

[13] She seeks wool and flax,
> And willingly works with her hands.

[14] She is like the merchant ships,
> She brings her food from afar.

[15] She also rises while it is yet night,
> And provides food for her household,
> And a portion for her maidservants.

[16] She considers a field and buys it;
> From her profits she plants a vineyard.

[17] She girds (prepares) herself with strength,
> And strengthens her arms.

[18] She perceives that her merchandise is good,
> And her lamp does not go out by night.

[19] She stretches out her hands to the distaff,
> And her hand holds the spindle
> (items used to spin flax or wool into thread and yarn).

[20] **She extends her hand to the poor,**
> **Yes, she reaches out her hands to the needy.**

[21] She is not afraid of snow for her household,
> For all her household is clothed with scarlet.

[22] She makes tapestry for herself;
> Her clothing is fine linen and purple.

[23] Her husband is known in the gates,
> When he sits among the elders of the land.

[24] She makes linen garments and sells them,
> And supplies sashes for the merchants.

[25] Strength and honor are her clothing;
> She shall rejoice in time to come.

²⁶ **She opens her mouth with wisdom,**
   And on her tongue is the law of kindness!
²⁷ She watches over the ways of her household,
   And does not eat the bread of idleness.
²⁸ Her children rise up and call her blessed;
   Her husband also, and he praises her:
²⁹ "Many daughters have done well,
   But you excel them all."
³⁰ **Charm is *deceitful* and beauty is *passing*,**
   But a woman who fears the LORD, she shall be *praised*!
³¹ Give her of the fruit of her hands,
   And let her own works praise her in the gates.

Wine

Your eyes will see strange things,
   And your heart *will* utter *perverse* things! (Proverbs 23:33)

Who has *woe*?
   Who has *sorrow*? Who has *contentions*?
   Who has *complaints*? Who has wounds without cause?
   Who has redness of eyes? (Proverbs 23:29)
Those who linger long at the wine,
   Those who go in search of mixed wine. (Proverbs 23:30)
Do not look on the wine when it is red,
   When it sparkles in the cup,
   When it swirls around smoothly; (Proverbs 23:31)
At the last it bites like a serpent,
   And stings like a viper. (Proverbs 23:32)
Your eyes will see strange things,
   And your heart *will* utter *perverse* things! (Proverbs 23:33)
Yes, you will be like one who lies down in the midst of the sea,
   Or like one who lies at the top of the mast, saying:
   "They have struck me, but I was not hurt;
   They have beaten me, but I did not feel it.
   When shall I awake, that I may seek another drink?" (Proverbs 23:34)
As a dog returns to his own vomit,
   So a fool *repeats* his folly! (Proverbs 26:11)

Wine is a mocker,
   Strong drink is a brawler,
   And whoever is led astray by it is *not* wise! (Proverbs 20:1)
Do not mix with winebibbers,
   Or with gluttonous eaters of meat; (Proverbs 23:20)
For the drunkard and the glutton will come to poverty,
   And drowsiness will clothe a man with rags. (Proverbs 23:21)
He who loves pleasure will be a poor man;
   He who loves wine and oil *will not be rich*! (Proverbs 21:17)
Whoever loves wisdom makes his father rejoice,
   But a companion of harlots *wastes* his wealth! (Proverbs 29:3)

It is not for kings, O Lemuel,
   It is not for kings to drink wine,
   Nor for princes intoxicating drink; (Proverbs 31:4)
Lest they drink and forget the law,
   And *pervert* the justice of all the afflicted. (Proverbs 31:5)
Give strong drink to him who is perishing,
   And wine to those who are bitter of heart. (Proverbs 31:6)
Let him drink and forget his poverty,
   And remember his misery no more. (Proverbs 31:7)

The King

It is an abomination for kings to commit wickedness. (Proverbs 16:12)

The Good King
The king's heart is in the hand of the LORD,
    Like the rivers of water;
    He turns it wherever He wishes. (Proverbs 21:1)
A king who sits on the throne of judgment
    Scatters all evil with his eyes. (Proverbs 20:8)
A wise king sifts out the wicked,
    And brings the threshing wheel over them. (Proverbs 20:26)
Divination is on the lips of the king;
    His mouth *must not* transgress in judgment. (Proverbs 16:10)
Excellent speech is not becoming to a fool,
    Much less lying lips to a prince. (Proverbs 17:7)
If a ruler pays attention to lies,
    All his servants become wicked. (Proverbs 29:12)
Righteous lips are the *delight* of kings,
    And they love him who speaks what is right. (Proverbs 16:13)
Mercy and truth preserve the king,
    And by loving kindness he upholds his throne. (Proverbs 20:28)
It is an abomination for kings to commit wickedness,
    For a throne is established by righteousness. (Proverbs 16:12)
When the righteous are in authority, the people rejoice;
    But when a wicked man rules, the people *groan*. (Proverbs 29:2)

The Absence of a Wise Ruler
Because of the transgression of a land, many are its princes;
    But by a man of understanding and knowledge
    Right will be prolonged. (Proverbs 28:2)
In a multitude of people is a king's honor,
    But in the lack of people is the downfall of a prince. (Proverbs 14:28)
Like a roaring lion and a charging bear
    Is a wicked ruler over poor people. (Proverbs 28:15)
Also, to punish the righteous is not good,
    Nor to strike princes for their uprightness. (Proverbs 17:26)

Many seek the ruler's favor,
> **But *justice* for man comes from the LORD!** (Proverbs 29:26)

A ruler who lacks understanding is a great oppressor,
> But he who hates covetousness (greed)
> Will prolong his days. (Proverbs 28:16)

When the wicked arise, men hide themselves;
> But when they perish, the righteous increase. (Proverbs 28:28)

The King's Wrath and Favor

As messengers of death is the king's wrath,
> But a wise man will appease it. (Proverbs 16:14)

In the light of the king's face is life,
> And his favor is like a cloud of the latter rain. (Proverbs 16:15)

The king's favor is toward a wise servant,
> But his wrath is against him who causes shame. (Proverbs 14:35)

The king's wrath is like the roaring of a lion,
> But his favor is like dew on the grass. (Proverbs 19:12)

The wrath of a king is like the roaring of a lion;
> **Whoever provokes [the king] to anger**
> **Sins against his own life!** (Proverbs 20:2)

My son, fear the LORD and the king;
> Do not associate with those given to change; (Proverbs 24:21)

For their calamity (great misfortune) will rise suddenly,
> And who knows the ruin
> > Those two (*the LORD and the king*) can bring? (Proverbs 24:22)

Friends of Rulers

He who loves purity of heart
> And has grace on his lips,
> > The king will be his friend. (Proverbs 22:11)

By long forbearance (self- restraint) a ruler is persuaded,
> And a gentle tongue breaks a bone. (Proverbs 25:15)

Dining With Rulers
When you sit down to eat with a ruler,
    Consider carefully what is before you; (Proverbs 23:1)
And put a knife to your throat
    If you are a man given to appetite. (Proverbs 23:2)
Do not desire his delicacies,
    For they are *deceptive* food! (Proverbs 23:3)

Further Wise Sayings of Solomon Concerning the King
These also are proverbs of Solomon
    Which the men of Hezekiah king of Judah copied: (Proverbs 25:1)
It is the glory of God to conceal a matter,
    But the glory of kings is to search out a matter. (Proverbs 25:2)
As the heavens for height and the earth for depth,
    So the heart of kings is unsearchable. (Proverbs 25:3)
Take away the dross (the slag from molten metal) from silver,
    And it will go to the silversmith for jewelry. (Proverbs 25:4)
Take away the wicked from before the king,
    And his throne will be established in righteousness. (Proverbs 25:5)
Do not exalt (lift up) yourself in the presence of the king,
    And do not stand in the place of the great; (Proverbs 25:6)
For it is better that he say to you,
   "Come up here,"
    Than that you should be put lower in the presence of the prince,
    Whom your eyes have seen. (Proverbs 25:7)
Like a bird that wanders from its nest
    Is a man who wanders from his place. (Proverbs 27:8)

The Words of King Lemuel
The words of King Lemuel,
    The utterance which his mother taught him: (Proverbs 31:1)
What, my son?
    And what, son of my womb?
    And what, son of my vows? (Proverbs 31:2)
Do not give your strength to women,
    Nor your ways to that which *destroys* kings. (Proverbs 31:3)

It is not for kings, O Lemuel,
> It is not for kings to drink wine,
> Nor for princes intoxicating drink; (Proverbs 31:4)

Lest they drink and forget the law,
> And *pervert* the justice
> Of all the afflicted (those who suffer). (Proverbs 31:5)

Give strong drink to him who is perishing,
> And wine to those who are bitter of heart. (Proverbs 31:6)

Let him drink and forget his poverty,
> And remember his misery no more. (Proverbs 31:7)

Open your mouth for the speechless,
> In the cause of all who are appointed to die. (Proverbs 31:8)

Open your mouth, judge righteously,
> And plead the cause of the poor and needy. (Proverbs 31:9)

The king who judges the poor with truth,
> **His throne will be established *forever*!** (Proverbs 29:14)

The Wisdom of Agur

The Man Without Wisdom
The words of Agur the son of Jakeh, his utterance.
    This man declared to Ithiel—to Ithiel and Ucal: (Proverbs 30:1)
Surely I am more stupid than any man,
    And do not have the understanding of a man. (Proverbs 30:2)
I neither learned wisdom
    Nor have knowledge of the Holy One. (Proverbs 30:3)
Who has ascended into heaven, or descended?
    Who has gathered the wind in His fists?
    Who has bound the waters in a garment?
    Who has established all the ends of the earth?
    What is His name, and what is His Son's name,
    If you know? (Proverbs 30:4)

Four Things Never Satisfied
There are three things that are never satisfied,
    Four never say, "Enough!" (Proverbs 30:15)
The grave,
    The barren womb,
    The earth that is not satisfied with water—
    And the fire never says, "Enough!" (Proverbs 30:16)

Four Things Beyond Understanding
There are three things which are too wonderful for me,
    Yes, four which I do not understand: (Proverbs 30:18)
The way of an eagle in the air,
    The way of a serpent on a rock,
    The way of a ship in the midst of the sea,
    And the way of a man with a virgin. (Proverbs 30:19)

Four Things Unbearable
For three things the earth is perturbed,
   Yes, for four it cannot bear up: (Proverbs 30:21)
For a servant when he reigns,
   A fool when he is filled with food, (Proverbs 30:22)
A hateful woman when she is married,
   And a maidservant who succeeds her mistress. (Proverbs 30:23)

Four Things Exceedingly Wise
There are four things which are little on the earth,
   But they are exceedingly wise: (Proverbs 30:24)
The ants are a people not strong,
   Yet they prepare their food in the summer; (Proverbs 30:25)
The rock badgers are a feeble folk,
   Yet they make their homes in the crags; (Proverbs 30:26)
The locusts have no king,
   Yet they all advance in ranks; (Proverbs 30:27)
The spider skillfully grasps with its hands,
   And it is in kings' palaces. (Proverbs 30:28)

Four Things Majestic
There are three things which are majestic in pace,
   Yes, four which are stately in walk: (Proverbs 30:29)
A lion, which is mighty among beasts
   And does not turn away from any; (Proverbs 30:30)
A greyhound,
   A male goat also,
   And a king whose troops are with him! (Proverbs 30:31)

Made in the USA
Columbia, SC
29 September 2024